# YOUR BELIEF SYSTEM

## HOW YOUR THOUGHTS DICTATE YOUR LIFE

By

Nick Imoru

**Achievers Publishing**
Calgary, Canada

**YOUR BELIEF SYSTEM: HOW YOUR THOUGHTS DICTATE YOUR LIFE**
Copyright © 2024 By Nicholas Imoru

ISBN: 978-1-989291-05-4

Published in Canada, by
**Achievers Publishing**

**Canadian Cataloguing in Publication (CIP)**
A Record of this Publication is available from the Library and Archives Canada (LAC).



For further information or permission, address:
**Achievers Publishing**
Calgary, Canada
E-mail: info@achieverspublishing.com
www.achieverspublishing.com

Printed in Canada for Achievers Publishing

# YOUR BELIEF SYSTEM

## HOW YOUR THOUGHTS DICTATE YOUR LIFE

# *Dedication*

To my beloved mother, Regina Imoru, who selflessly sacrificed for me and my 11 siblings. Your love, strength, and tireless dedication continue to be the foundation of our lives. This book is a testament to the values and lessons you've instilled in each of us. I am forever grateful for your unwavering support, faith, and courage.

Thank you, Mama, for everything.

# Table of Contents

Contents


*Dedication* ......................................................... 5

*Table of Contents* ............................................... 7

*Introduction* ..................................................... 13

*Chapter 1* ........................................................ 15

**CASE STUDY – THE LION** .............................. 15

   Some Essential Facts About Lions ................... 16

*Chapter 2* ........................................................ 19

**WHAT IS A BELIEF-SYSTEM?** ......................... 19

   Belief System and Its Influence ..................... 20

*Chapter 3* ........................................................ 25

**BELIEFS, SCIENCE, KNOWLEDGE & VALUES** ..... 25

   Belief System & Science ............................... 25

   Beliefs v Knowledge .................................... 27

   What is Knowledge? ..................................... 30

   The Sources of Knowledge ............................ 31

   How Belief Systems Influence Knowledge ........ 34

   Beliefs And Values ....................................... 34

*Chapter 4* ........................................................ 37

**HOW BELIEF-SYSTEM WORK** .......................... 37

   Why is Your Belief System Important? ............ 37

How Belief-Systems Work: Natural Wheel of Belief.........................38

Example of the Belief Cycle in Action ...........................................41

Key Takeaways from the Beliefs' Cycle..........................................44

Changing the Cycle.....................................................................45

*Chapter 5* ...............................................................................49

**BELIEFS & ATTITUDE**.............................................................49

Where Do Your Attitude Come From? ...........................................51

The Power of Your Mindset .........................................................53

*Chapter 6* ...............................................................................57

**HOW DO WE FORM OR CREATE OUR BELIEF-SYSTEM?** ...............57

The Two Kinds of Belief: Information-Based & Faith-Based ..............59

   1.    Information-Based Beliefs ..........................................59

   2.    Faith-Based Beliefs .....................................................60

Can Faith-Based Beliefs Be Proven Wrong? ..................................61

*Chapter 7* ...............................................................................63

**BELIEFS & FAITH** ..................................................................63

True Faith - Confident Attitude Toward God....................................65

Faith and Belief: Two Sides of the Same Coin ................................66

*Chapter 8* ...............................................................................69

**BELIEFS & PHILOSOPHY** ........................................................69

What is an Idea?........................................................................70

*Chapter 9* ...............................................................................73

**THE CONCEPT OF SPIRIT, SOUL & BODY** ..................................73

The Spirit..................................................................................76

The Soul ...................................................................................77

The Body...................................................................................77

The Workings of the Spirit, the Soul, and the Body ...................... 80

The Battle of the Soul ........................................................ 84

The Battle of the Soul ........................................................ 91

*Chapter 10* ...................................................................... 99

**THE CONCEPT OF THE MIND** .......................................... 99

Aspects of the Mind ........................................................ 100

Key Differentiations ........................................................ 101

The Power of the Human Mind .......................................... 102

Classification of the Mind ................................................ 103

   1.    The Conscious Mind .............................................. 103

   2.    The Subconscious (Preconscious) Mind ...................... 104

   3.    The Unconscious Mind ........................................... 105

*Chapter 11* ...................................................................... 107

**THE POWER OF THE SUBCONSCIOUS MIND & ITS ROLE IN BELIEF SYSTEMS** ................................................................ 107

Subconscious Mind as a Memory Bank ................................ 107

Why Is the Subconscious Mind More Powerful? .................... 108

The Functions of the Subconscious Mind ............................ 110

*Chapter 12* ...................................................................... 115

**HOW DO OUR BELIEFS DRIVE US?** ................................ 115

Beliefs and the Subconscious Mind .................................... 115

How Our Beliefs Shape Our Lives ...................................... 116

The Power of Emotion in Reinforcing Beliefs ........................ 117

Breaking the Cycle .......................................................... 118

Taking Responsibility for Our Beliefs .................................. 118

*Chapter 13* ...................................................................... 121

**YOU ARE A VICTIM OF YOUR BELIEFS** .......................... 121

The Power of Belief in Shaping Your Life ............................................. 122

Reprogramming Your Belief System ................................................... 122

How to Change Your Belief System ................................................... 123

*Chapter 14* ............................................................................... 125

**SELF-CONCEPT** ....................................................................... 125

The 3 Components of Self-Concept ................................................... 128

    1.    Self-Image ..................................................... 130

    2.    Self-Esteem or Self-Worth ............................. 134

    3.    Real-Self ....................................................... 139

High-Level Summary ....................................................................... 141

*Chapter 15* ............................................................................... 145

**SELF-IDENTITY** ....................................................................... 145

Who Are You? ............................................................................... 145

    1.    Created in the Image and Likeness of God ..... 148

    2.    Uniquely and Wonderfully Made by God ....... 150

    3.    Given Dominion Over the Whole Earth ......... 151

    4.    The Highest of God's Creation ..................... 152

*Chapter 16* ............................................................................... 155

**HOW TO REPROGRAM YOUR BELIEFS SYSTEM** ........................... 155

Your Mindset ............................................................................... 156

Anatomy of the Human Mind .......................................................... 158

Technique to Reprogram the Subconscious Mind .............................. 163

*Chapter 17* ............................................................................... 169

**RECOGNIZE THE PROBLEM** ....................................................... 169

Analyzing Your Responses .............................................................. 173

Taking Action ............................................................................... 174

*Chapter 18* ......................................................................................... 177

**THINK GOD'S THOUGHTS** ............................................................. 177

Have the Mind of Christ.................................................................. 177

New Creation Reality...................................................................... 178

The Indwell of the Holy Spirit ........................................................ 183

Partakers of the Divine Nature ...................................................... 184

Taking Every Thought Captive ....................................................... 188

*Chapter 19* ......................................................................................... 196

**VISUALIZATION**............................................................................. 196

Understanding Visualization ......................................................... 204

Biblical Foundation of Visualization .............................................. 205

The Power of the Mind in Visualization ......................................... 206

How to Practice Visualization........................................................ 206

*Chapter 20* ......................................................................................... 209

**POSITIVE AFFIRMATIONS** ............................................................ 209

What Are Affirmations? ................................................................. 213

How to Create Effective Affirmations............................................. 213

How to Use Affirmations Effectively .............................................. 214

The Power of Affirmations ............................................................. 215

*Chapter 21* ......................................................................................... 217

**POSITIVE SELF-TALK**.................................................................... 217

Importance of Positive Self-Talk ................................................... 219

How to Create the Habit of Positive Self-Talk in Your Daily Life......222

The Power of Self-Talk:.................................................................. 226

How Positive Self-Talk Works: ...................................................... 227

Practical Steps to Implement Positive Self-Talk:........................... 228

The Impact of Positive Self-Talk:................................................... 230

The Importance of Positive Self-Talk: ........................................... 231

Practical Application of Positive Self-Talk: ...................................232

*Chapter 22* ............................................................................. 237

**GRATITUDE AND APPRECIATION** ...................................... 237

Benefits of Gratitude: .........................................................239

An Expression of Autonomy ..............................................241

How to Cultivate an Attitude of Gratitude............................243

*Chapter 23* ............................................................................. 257

**CREATE A VISION BOARD (DREAM BOARD)** .................... 257

The Biblical Foundation for a Vision Board .........................257

How a Vision Board Reprograms Your Belief System...........258

Steps to Create a Vision Board...........................................259

Benefits of a Vision Board .................................................261

*Chapter 24* ............................................................................. 265

**MEDITATION** ..................................................................... 265

Engage the Power of the Mind ...........................................267

The Role of Meditation in Reprogramming .........................272

Steps to Effective Meditation for Reprogramming................273

*Conclusion* .............................................................................. 275

*About the Author* .................................................................... 277

*Books by the Same Author* ...................................................... 279

# *Introduction*

What if I told you that the quality of your life is not merely the result of chance, fate, or circumstance, but rather a direct reflection of your beliefs? Your belief system—the set of ideas, principles, and convictions you hold—shapes your reality more profoundly than you might realize. From the decisions you make to the way you perceive the world; your beliefs are the driving force behind every outcome you experience.

This book, *Your Belief System: How Your Thoughts Dictate Your Life*, is an exploration of the powerful role that beliefs play in determining the course of your life. It delves into how your thoughts, rooted in these beliefs, create the mental framework that governs your emotions, actions, and ultimately, your destiny.

Throughout these pages, we will unpack the concept of a belief system, examining its influence on various aspects of life, including your attitudes, mindset, and self-identity. We'll explore how belief systems are formed, the interplay between beliefs and knowledge, and the critical role that faith plays in shaping your reality. You'll learn how your beliefs are like seeds planted in the subconscious mind, growing into the thoughts, feelings, and actions that define your existence.

In understanding how belief systems operate, you will gain the tools to transform your life from the inside out. By identifying and reshaping limiting beliefs, you can break free from negative cycles and create a new, empowering reality. Whether it's through changing your self-concept, reprogramming your subconscious mind, or cultivating a positive attitude, this book provides practical strategies for harnessing the power of your beliefs to achieve the success and fulfillment you desire.

As you embark on this journey, remember that your belief system is the foundation of your life's outcomes. What you believe about yourself and the world around you will manifest in your experiences. This truth underscores the importance of consciously cultivating beliefs that align with the life you want to lead.

Prepare to challenge your current beliefs, embrace new perspectives, and unlock the potential within you. The thoughts you choose to nurture today will shape the life you live tomorrow. Let's begin this transformative journey together.

# *Chapter 1*

# CASE STUDY – THE LION

After an excursion tour in Africa, I had the opportunity to see this majestic species—the lion—up close, and believe me, it was an unforgettable, spine-tingling experience.

Although the lion is often called the "King of the Jungle," it actually lives in grasslands, plains, and savannahs. I believe the expression "King of the Jungle" likely stems from a common misconception that Africa is entirely covered in jungles—a myth that is inaccurate. Alternatively, the phrase "King of the Jungle" may refer to a broader interpretation of the word "jungle," representing a wild or untamed environment.

Lions are universally recognized as symbols of strength, power, ferocity, and courage. Throughout history, they have been celebrated for these traits and are often associated with royalty and dignity, hence the phrase "King of the Jungle."

However, the focus here is to use this fearless and awe-inspiring creature as a case study in understanding the power of belief systems.

The lion is regarded as the "King of the Jungle" not because of its size, strength, or habitat, but because of its attitude. Attitude is a product of belief. The lion believes certain things about itself, which fundamentally shapes the way it behaves.

When the lion encounters other animals, it does not feel fear because of its belief system. The lion's confidence in its own identity allows it to act with authority and assurance. This is how its attitude is formed—by the beliefs it holds about itself.

## Some Essential Facts About Lions

To better understand this incredible creature, I've outlined 20 amazing facts about lions:

1. Lions are the second largest big cat species in the world, behind tigers.
2. The average male lion weighs around 180 kg (400 lb), while the average female weighs around 130 kg (290 lb).
3. The heaviest lion on record weighed an astonishing 375 kg (826 lb).
4. In the wild, lions typically live for an average of 12 years, though they can live up to 16 years. In captivity, they may live up to 25 years.
5. The mane of a male lion is a unique characteristic among big cats. It makes the lion appear larger, signals sexual maturity, and conveys health status.

6. Lions hunt large prey such as zebra and wildebeest.

7. Lions usually live in groups of 10 to 15 animals, known as prides.

8. They are the only big cat species that live in groups, and prides are close-knit family units.

9. Lionesses are better hunters than males and handle 85-90% of the pride's hunting, while males patrol the territory and protect the pride.

10. Lions work as a group and use intelligent hunting tactics to catch prey that would be too fast or challenging for a solo hunt.

11. Male lions defend the pride's territory, but despite the lionesses doing most of the hunting, the males eat first.

12. Lions can reach speeds of up to 81 kmph (50 mph), though only in short bursts due to limited stamina.

13. A lion can leap as far as 36 feet.

14. Lions walk without their heels touching the ground.

15. Lions roar to communicate their position to other prides; an adult male lion's roar can be heard up to 8 km (5 miles) away.

16. Lions have a highly developed range of communicative behaviors and expressive movements.

17. A female lion requires 5 kg of meat a day, while a male needs 7 kg or more daily.

18. Lions primarily hunt from dusk till dawn.

19. In the wild, lions spend between 16 and 20 hours a day resting and sleeping. Due to their limited sweat glands,

they conserve energy by resting during the heat of the day and become more active at night.

20. Lions possess remarkable night vision, being six times more sensitive to light than humans. This gives them a distinct advantage over prey during nocturnal hunts.

Because the lion understands these abilities, it has developed an uncommon attitude, making it a daring and fearless creature. This same understanding shapes the way the lion carries itself and behaves in its environment. The ultimate question is why? To answer this correctly, we must first understand what a belief system is.

# Chapter 2

# WHAT IS A BELIEF-SYSTEM?

The term "belief system" consists of two words: "belief" and "system." For a better understanding, I'd like to define each separately before constructing a complete meaning of the phrase "belief system."

In the context of our discussion, "yourdictionary.com" defines *belief* and *system* as follows:

## Belief

- The mental act, condition, or habit of placing trust or confidence in another.
- The mental acceptance and conviction in the truth, actuality, or validity of something.
- Something believed or accepted as true, especially a particular tenet or a body of tenets accepted by a group of people.
- Mental acceptance of a claim as likely true.
- Faith or trust in the reality of something, often based upon one's own reasoning, trust in a claim, desire for actuality, and/or evidence considered.

## System

- A set of facts, principles, or rules classified or arranged in a regular, orderly form to show a logical plan linking various parts.
- An established way of doing something; method; procedure.
- An organized set of interrelated ideas or principles.

Now, having explored the definitions of these two words, we can address a common misconception about the meaning of "belief system." Many people tend to immediately associate belief systems with "religious stuff"—collection of ideas with a religious foundation. Others, as defined by "collinsdictionary.com," believe:

*The belief system of a person or society is the set of beliefs they have about what is right and wrong, or what is true and false.*

While this definition captures some truth, it only reflects part of the picture. A belief system is not solely about determining what is right or wrong, or true or false. It is much more comprehensive.

## Belief System and Its Influence

The Greek word for "belief" is *Pistis*, which means "confidence" or "trust." Interestingly, this is the same word used for "faith." Therefore, a belief system is not just a religious tenet or creed—it's far more encompassing. It defines who we are and shapes our identity. No one can rise above their belief system because it acts as the framework of ideas through which an individual makes sense of the world.

I appreciate how Deborah Teasley explains it: "*A belief system is an ideology or set of principles that helps us to interpret our everyday reality.*" Ideology refers to a set of beliefs or principles. Now, you may be wondering—aren't these the same thing? Not quite. Belief systems extend beyond mere ideologies. They act as an umbrella term, encompassing religions, philosophies, science, and more. In other words, belief systems are broader, while ideologies represent specific types of belief systems, such as existentialism in philosophy, which emphasizes free will and personal responsibility.

Given this understanding, I offer the following working definition of belief system:

*A belief system is a set of facts, ideas, principles, or rules through which we build faith or trust in the reality of something—often based upon our reasoning, trust in a claim, desire for actuality, or considered evidence. This belief system drives us to interpret, react to, and make sense of the world, ultimately dictating the direction of our lives, for better or worse.*

Our belief systems can manifest in the form of religion, spirituality, philosophy, or political affiliation. These beliefs are shaped by various factors—upbringing, knowledge, religious affiliation, and even peer pressure—all of which help to form, evolve, or even change our belief systems. As a result, we develop certain convictions that we rely on to navigate, interpret, and find meaning in the world, as well as to define our role and purpose within it.

To summarize, here are four key elements to understanding a belief system based on our working definition:

1. **Faith in Reality:** We build our faith or trust in the reality of something—whether it's religion, spirituality, philosophy, or politics—through a set of:
   - **Facts:** Knowledge or information based on real occurrences.
   - **Ideas:** Products of mental activity, such as thoughts or conceptions.
   - **Principles:** Basic truths or fundamental assumptions that form moral or ethical standards.
   - **Rules:** Established practices that serve as guides to behavior or understanding.
2. **Foundation of Faith:** This faith or trust is often built upon:
   - Our own reasoning
   - Trust in a claim
   - Desire for actuality

- Considered evidence

3. **Development of Convictions:** These convictions, formed by our belief system, guide how we interpret, react to, and make sense of the world around us.

4. **Impact on Life Direction:** Whether we realize it or not, the beliefs we hold and the convictions we develop have the power to dictate the course of our lives—for good or bad.

# Chapter 3

# BELIEFS, SCIENCE, KNOWLEDGE & VALUES

## Belief System & Science

Here's a provocative question to ponder on: Is science a belief system?

Many people would argue that:

- Science is rational, based on reason, and supported by evidence. As a result, it often stands in contrast to religious beliefs.
- Science is built on facts, whereas belief systems are rooted in faith.

However, I would argue yes—science can be seen as a belief system. You might ask, why?

If we return to our working definition of belief system, which describes it as "a set of facts, ideas, principles, or rules through which we build faith or trust in the reality of something," then science indeed fits this description. Science is based on facts, evidence, and repeatable experiments, but it still operates within a framework of belief—belief in certain principles, methodologies, and paradigms. As such, science can be considered a belief system.

It is essential to remember that scientists are human beings, subject to personal biases, emotions, and goals. These human factors inevitably influence their work, even when they strive for objectivity. The personal views and career ambitions of scientists can subtly shape the conclusions they draw, the experiments they conduct, and the hypotheses they favor.

Moreover, science operates within established paradigms—a set of accepted ideas and frameworks that guide research and interpretation of data. When new evidence arises that challenges these paradigms, it is often met with resistance. But if the challenges persist and accumulate, they may eventually lead to a paradigm shift. For example, for centuries, scientists believed that the earth was at the center of the universe (geocentrism). It wasn't until the heliocentric model, which placed the sun at the center, became widely accepted that this belief was overturned.

Recognizing that science is a belief system helps broaden our understanding of belief systems as a whole. It dismantles the notion that belief systems are solely based on faith or religion, thereby expanding the concept beyond "religious stuff." Our working definition shows that belief systems are deeply ingrained in various aspects of life, including science, philosophy, politics, and more.

This distinction is important. Understanding science as a belief system underscores how deeply interconnected our lives are with the belief systems we adopt—whether those systems are religious, scientific, or philosophical. Belief systems shape our perceptions, influence our decisions, and ultimately, dictate how we interpret and interact with the world.

The idea that science is purely fact-based and separate from belief diminishes the role belief systems play in shaping our understanding of reality. When we accept that science, like religion or philosophy, is rooted in a set of ideas, principles, and assumptions, we come to a fuller realization of how our belief systems govern our lives, not just in religious matters but across all domains of thought and action.

## Beliefs v Knowledge

Let's explore some commonly held distinctions between belief and knowledge:

- **Belief** is often viewed as something we think may be true.
- **Knowledge** is something we have proof of or evidence to back up.
- **Belief** involves a degree of doubt or uncertainty.
- **Knowledge** involves facts and certainty.

Philosophers have long debated the relationship between belief and knowledge. According to *Theaetetus* (a work by Plato), *"Knowledge is a subset of that which is both true and believed."* This notion is often illustrated using an **Euler diagram**, which represents sets and their relationships diagrammatically. In this context, the set of "belief" overlaps with the set of "truth," and where they intersect is what we call "knowledge."

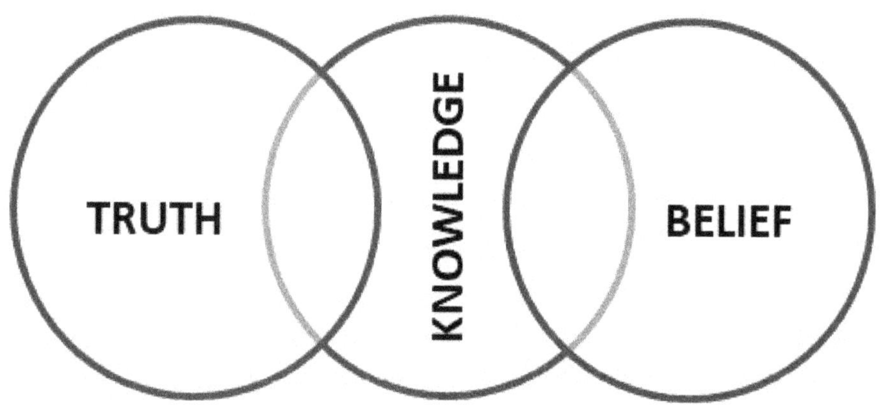


**Euler Diagram of Belief, Truth, and Knowledge**

- **Belief:** This set includes everything that a person considers to be true, but it may or may not actually be true.
- **Truth:** This set includes all statements that are factually correct, regardless of whether anyone believes them.
- **Knowledge:** The intersection of the two sets—where belief and truth overlap—is where knowledge lies. When we believe something that is both true and supported by evidence or facts, it becomes knowledge.

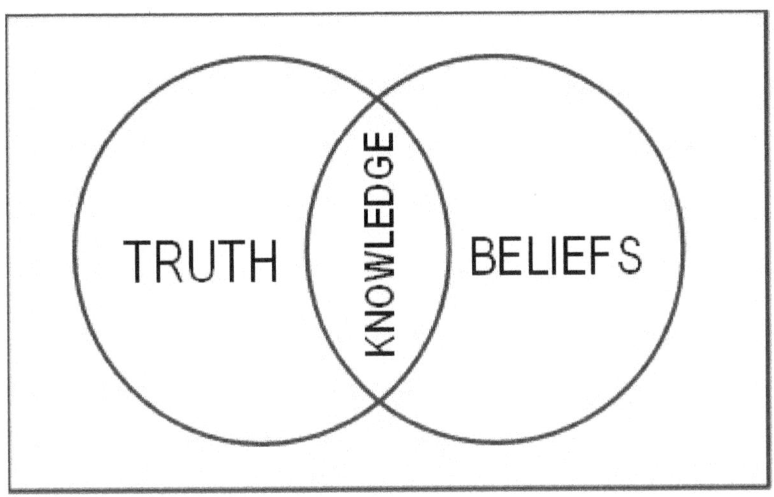


## The Philosophical Perspective: Epistemology

In philosophy, the study of knowledge is called epistemology. One of the most famous definitions of knowledge comes from Plato, who described knowledge as "justified true belief." According to this view, for a belief to be considered knowledge, it must meet three criteria:

1.  It must be true (aligned with reality).
2.  It must be believed (the individual accepts it as true).
3.  It must be justified (there is sufficient evidence or reasoning to support it).

## Shifting from Belief to Knowledge

Belief ceases to involve doubt when it is justified as truth. Once a belief has been proven to be true, it transitions into the realm of **knowledge**. This is why beliefs formed in childhood, which may have been based on limited information or misconceptions, can later be challenged or disproven as we grow older and acquire more knowledge.

For example, you may have believed something as a child because it was taught to you by trusted adults. However, as you gain access to more information and evidence, you may realize that this belief was not grounded in reality. In that case, the belief would not qualify as knowledge because it was not true, even though you held it with conviction at the time.

In summary, beliefs and knowledge are closely related but distinct. Beliefs often involve some degree of uncertainty or personal conviction, while knowledge is characterized by certainty, truth, and justification. As we acquire new information and evidence, our beliefs can either be reinforced and transformed into knowledge or challenged and discarded.

## What is Knowledge?

According to Wikipedia, knowledge is *"a familiarity, awareness, or understanding of someone or something, such as **facts, information, descriptions, or skills**, which is acquired through **experience** or **education** by **perceiving, discovering, or learning.**"* This definition underscores that knowledge involves both the accumulation of facts and the deeper understanding gained through active engagement with those facts.

## The Sources of Knowledge

It is often said that "knowledge is power," but this isn't entirely accurate. The power comes from **applied knowledge**—the knowledge that is put to use. Knowledge that is never applied remains inert, but knowledge that is utilized can have tremendous power and effect. The key question then becomes: How do we acquire knowledge?

There are two principal ways through which knowledge can be acquired: **Experience** and **Education**.

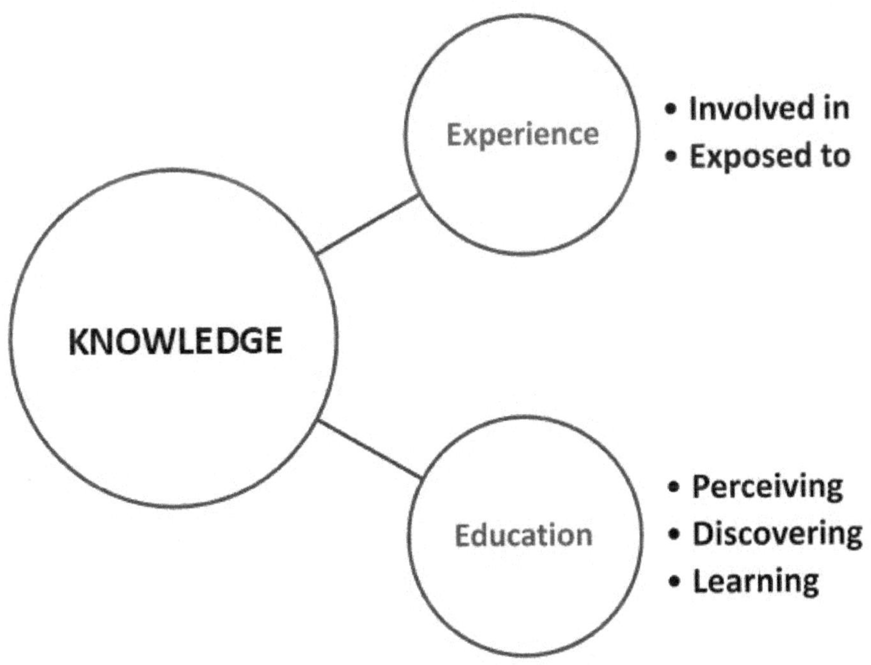

# 1. Experience

**Experience** refers to the firsthand effects or influence of an event or subject gained through direct involvement or exposure. Experience does not necessarily imply long-term learning or the acquisition of skills, though these are often associated with it. Experience is the act of living through events or participating in activities, leading to the accumulation of knowledge or skill.

- **Active Participation:** This refers to being directly involved in the act or event.
- **Observation or Exposure:** This refers to gaining knowledge through indirect means, such as observing or being exposed to an event without active participation.

Thus, experience is the first principal way of acquiring knowledge.

# 2. Education

**Education** is the process of facilitating learning or the acquisition of knowledge, skills, values, beliefs, and habits. Educational methods include teaching, training, storytelling, discussion, and directed research. Education can take place in both formal settings, like schools and universities, and informal settings, such as life experiences or self-study.

There are three primary ways by which education is acquired: **Perception**, **Discovery**, and **Learning**.

- **Perception:** This is the insight or knowledge gained by thinking. It involves using one's mental faculties to grasp objects, qualities, or concepts by means of the senses, awareness, comprehension, insight, or intuition.
- **Discovery:** Discovery involves detecting something new or previously unrecognized. In science and academia, it often refers to observing new phenomena or events and providing new reasoning to explain them using previously acquired knowledge.
- **Learning:** Learning is the process of acquiring new understanding, behaviors, skills, values, and preferences. It is an ongoing process that starts at birth and continues until death, shaped by interactions between individuals and their environment.

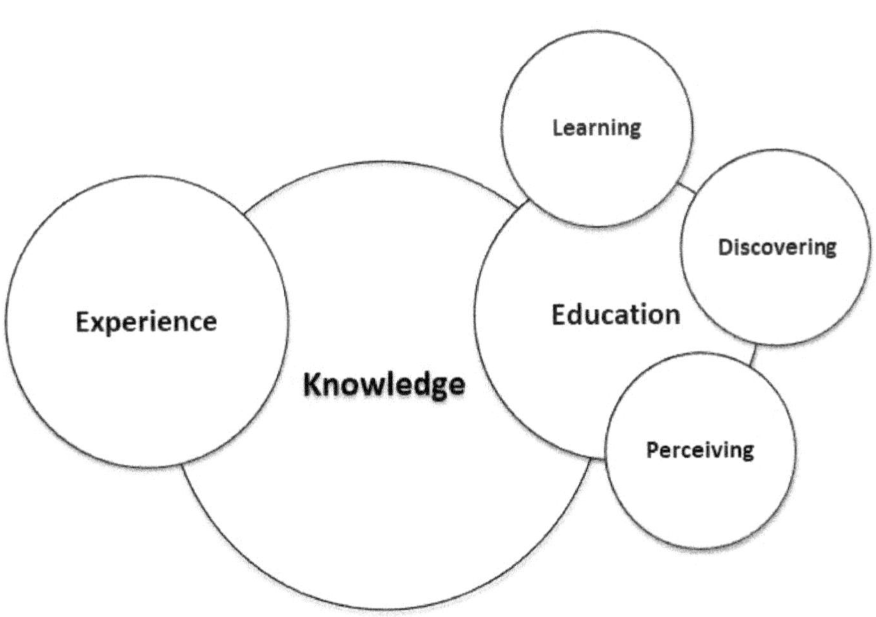

## How Belief Systems Influence Knowledge

An interesting aspect of knowledge acquisition is that it is not entirely objective. The **belief system** of an individual influences how they acquire and interpret knowledge. A **belief system** is a set of principles, facts, ideas, or rules that people use to understand and make sense of the world. It influences how we perceive reality, how we react to it, and how we internalize new information.

Even if two people are exposed to the same information, their takeaway or understanding can differ because of their unique belief systems. Their existing beliefs act as filters, affecting how they interpret and integrate new knowledge, regardless of its objective truth.

In conclusion, knowledge can be acquired through **experience** or **education**, but it is always filtered through the lens of our belief systems. These belief systems shape our perceptions, understandings, and reactions to new information. Therefore, knowledge is not just a simple accumulation of facts, but a dynamic process influenced by personal experience, education, and pre-existing beliefs.

## Beliefs And Values

Values are essentially a collection of guiding principles that influence what one deems to be correct and desirable in life, especially regarding personal conduct. They represent the moral compass that steers our decisions and actions. These values are deeply ingrained within us—often forming part of our DNA, so to speak—and they shape our very essence as individuals.

Values are the bedrock upon which our beliefs are built. These beliefs, in turn, guide our behavior in life, influencing how we respond to situations, how we interact with others, and how we approach the challenges and opportunities that come our way. Our values and beliefs work together to form the framework that governs not only our actions but also our relationships, our aspirations, and our overall worldview.

In the subsequent chapters, we will delve deeper into the relationship between values and beliefs and explore how these foundational principles shape every aspect of our lives—how we think, how we act, and how we engage with the world around us. Understanding this connection is critical for personal growth, success, and fulfillment in all areas of life.

*Chapter 4*

# HOW BELIEF-SYSTEM WORK

When we examine our lives, it becomes evident that our belief systems are constantly at work, shaping our reality. Our belief systems govern how we perceive the world, react to events, interact with others, and approach challenges. They determine our health, relationships, success, and overall well-being. Simply put, our belief system rules our life.

## Why is Your Belief System Important?

- **Your belief system rules your life.**
- **If you fail or succeed, it is because of your belief system.** Your beliefs influence your mindset and behaviors, which in turn shape your outcomes.
- **Your belief system causes you to think and feel the way you do.** Whether you are depressed, happy, sad, excited, or bored, your beliefs are the root cause.
- **Your belief system drives your actions.** It dictates your behaviors and decisions, ultimately influencing the course of your life.

- **Your belief system is the source of both positive and negative experiences.** It is responsible for the love, joy, and success you experience, as well as the hatred, frustration, and stress.
- **Your belief system determines your courage, fears, and overall behavior.**
- **Your belief system functions as the "auto-pilot" of your life.** It automatically controls your life's outcomes, whether you're aware of it or not.

## How Belief-Systems Work: Natural Wheel of Belief

Our beliefs are like seeds planted in our subconscious mind, growing into thoughts, feelings, actions, and results that shape our reality. To understand how belief systems work, we can examine the **Natural Wheel of Belief**—a cycle that explains the continuous flow of influence between our beliefs, thoughts, feelings, actions, and outcomes (results).

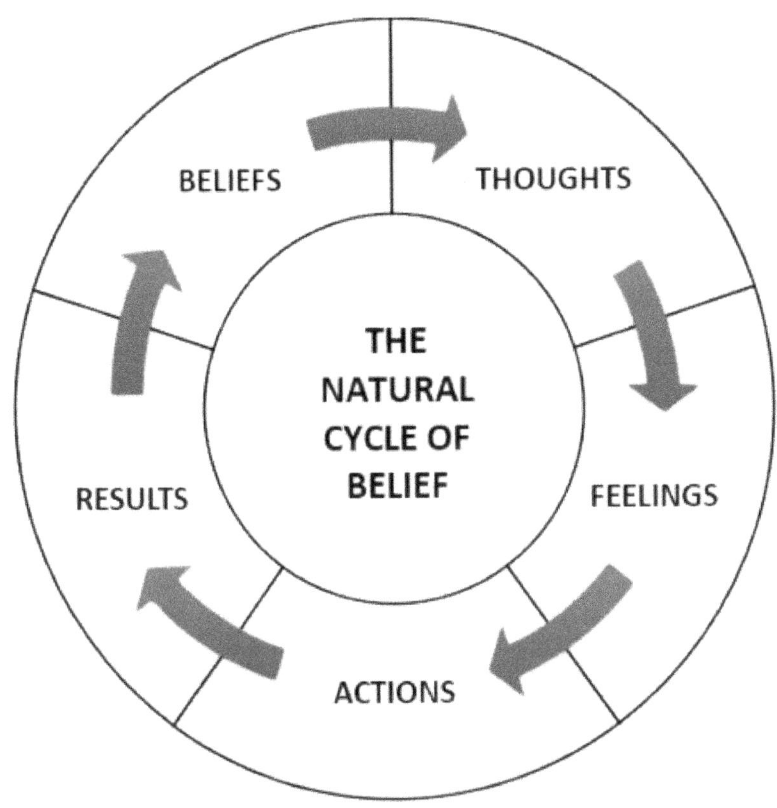


**The Natural Wheel of Belief**

1.  **Belief:** It all begins with a belief. Your belief can be about anything—your capabilities, your worth, the nature of the world, etc. This belief shapes your reality.

2.  **Thoughts:** Your belief generates specific thoughts. These thoughts are shaped by the belief you hold and begin to dictate your mental state.

3.  **Feelings:** Your thoughts cause you to experience particular feelings. For example, if you believe you are capable of success, you will feel confident; if you

believe you are destined to fail, you will feel anxious or fearful.

4. **Actions:** Your feelings lead to actions. The way you feel influences your behavior and the choices you make. Positive feelings drive productive actions, while negative feelings often result in self-sabotage or inaction.

5. **Results:** Your actions produce results. These results are a reflection of the beliefs, thoughts, and feelings that initiated them. If your belief is empowering, you will see positive results. If it is disempowering, your results will reflect that.

6. **Reinforcement:** The results you experience further reinforce your initial belief. If the results align with your belief, the belief is strengthened. If they do not, you may begin to question and alter your belief system.

The cycle then continues, creating a self-perpetuating loop. Every result feeds back into your belief system, either solidifying it or challenging it to evolve. This cycle explains why change is often difficult—our deeply ingrained beliefs create a loop that can be hard to break. However, by becoming aware of this cycle, you can intentionally alter your beliefs and transform the outcomes in your life.

## Example of the Belief Cycle in Action

Let's take the example of a person who is overweight and wants to lose weight. However, their initial belief is that they can't do anything at the gym, that they won't be able to keep up, and that they are likely to get hurt while working out. This belief is the starting point in the belief cycle.

1.  **Belief:** "I can't do anything at the gym."
2.  **Thought:** This belief generates thoughts of inadequacy and fear: "I'm going to get hurt," or "I won't be able to keep up."
3.  **Feeling:** These thoughts produce feelings of discouragement, anxiety, and low self-esteem.
4.  **Action:** The action that follows is avoidance of the gym. The person doesn't work out or take steps to lose weight.
5.  **Result:** The result of not taking action is continued weight gain or failure to lose weight.
6.  **Reinforcement:** The outcome (weight gain) reinforces the initial belief that the person is incapable of working out or losing weight, thus continuing the cycle.

This cycle will continue until the person changes their belief.

Now, consider a different scenario:

1.  **Belief:** "I can do anything at the gym, and I won't get hurt."

2. **Thought:** This positive belief generates empowering thoughts like, "I'm capable of achieving my goals," or "I can take it one step at a time."

3. **Feeling:** The thoughts create feelings of confidence and determination, even if the person knows it won't be easy.

4. **Action:** The person takes action by going to the gym for the first time.

5. **Result:** By showing up and taking action, they start seeing progress in their fitness and weight loss.

6. **Reinforcement:** This positive result reinforces their belief in their ability to work out and lose weight, and the cycle continues in a positive direction.

The difference between the two scenarios is the belief. The beliefs influence the thoughts, which create feelings, drive actions, and produce results. If you want to change your results, you must start by changing your belief. The belief is the foundation for the entire cycle.

## How to Change Your Belief Cycle

If you want to effect change in your life, the belief cycle offers a remedy. You need to identify the point in the cycle where change is needed and trace it back to its origin.

- **Step 1:** Identify the result you're dissatisfied with. For instance, feeling depressed or not achieving a goal.

- **Step 2:** Trace the result back to the action. What actions (or lack of action) are contributing to this result?
- **Step 3:** Examine the feelings behind your actions. What emotions are driving or hindering your behavior?
- **Step 4:** Reflect on the thoughts creating those emotions. What are you telling yourself?
- **Step 5:** Dig deeper into the belief that is generating those thoughts. What belief is at the core?

Once you've identified the belief, you can work on changing it. For example, if you're feeling depressed, recognize that your thoughts are creating those feelings. If you replace negative thoughts with more positive or empowering thoughts, your feelings will begin to shift, and with them, your actions and results will change as well.

## Application to Any Area of Life

This belief cycle applies to every area of life—career, finances, relationships, and even parenting. No matter the context, if you want a different result, start by addressing the belief behind it.

By consciously identifying and altering the beliefs driving your cycle, you can break free from limiting patterns and create new, empowering cycles that lead to the success, happiness, and fulfillment you desire.

In summary, the Natural Wheel of Belief shows that: *Our beliefs create our thoughts. and those thoughts create feelings. and those feelings create actions. and those actions create results.*

## Key Takeaways from the Beliefs' Cycle

This example beautifully illustrates the power of belief systems and how they impact our lives. The beliefs' cycle shows that everything starts with a belief, which influences our thoughts, feelings, actions, and, ultimately, our results. Whether positive or negative, our beliefs shape the outcomes we experience.

1. **Beliefs Shape Thoughts:** The belief you hold sets the stage for your thought process. If you believe you can achieve something, your thoughts will align with that belief, creating a mental environment that encourages success. Conversely, if you believe you can't do something, your thoughts will reflect that limitation, creating self-doubt and fear.

2. **Thoughts Generate Feelings:** Your thoughts have a powerful effect on your emotions. Positive beliefs lead to thoughts that create positive feelings such as confidence, motivation, and optimism. Negative beliefs create thoughts that produce feelings of inadequacy, fear, and anxiety.

3. **Feelings Influence Actions:** How you feel dictates the actions you take. When you feel empowered, you are more likely to take bold and constructive actions. When you feel discouraged, you may avoid taking any action or engage in behaviors that reinforce your negative beliefs.

4. **Actions Produce Results:** Your actions directly determine the results you achieve. Positive actions lead to positive outcomes, while negative or avoidant actions lead to stagnation or failure.

5. **Results Reinforce Beliefs:** The results you achieve then reinforce your original beliefs, completing the cycle. Positive results strengthen your belief in your ability to succeed, while negative results may reinforce a belief in your limitations.

## Changing the Cycle

If you want to change your life, start by changing your beliefs. As demonstrated in the example, once you shift your belief system, your thoughts, feelings, actions, and results will follow suit.

## Practical Application:

1. **Identify the Belief:** Begin by identifying the belief that is holding you back. In the example, it was the belief

that the gym was a dangerous place, leading to fear of injury and avoidance. Recognize the limiting belief.

2.  **Challenge the Belief:** Replace the limiting belief with a more empowering one. For example, change "I will get hurt at the gym" to "I can safely work out and get stronger."

3.  **Reframe Your Thoughts:** Begin thinking thoughts that align with your new belief. Instead of thinking, "I can't do this," start telling yourself, "I am capable of achieving this goal."

4.  **Embrace New Feelings:** As you change your thoughts, you will notice your feelings shifting. Feelings of inadequacy and fear will be replaced by confidence and determination.

5.  **Take Action:** Based on your new belief and feelings, take action that supports your goals. If it's working out, go to the gym and engage in activities that reflect your new belief.

6.  **Experience New Results:** These actions will lead to positive results that further reinforce your belief in your ability to succeed.

**The Power of Awareness:**

The beliefs' cycle can either trap you in a loop of negative outcomes or propel you toward success and fulfillment. The key is awareness. By becoming aware of the beliefs driving your actions, you can take control of the cycle and consciously create the life you want.

To effect lasting change, start at the root: your belief system. By doing so, you can transform your thoughts, emotions, actions, and ultimately, your reality.

# Chapter 5

# BELIEFS & ATTITUDE

In Chapter 1, we explored how the lion's understanding of its abilities leads to an uncommon attitude that makes it a daring creature. This attitude stems from the lion's belief system—its confidence in its own strengths and capabilities, which informs how it behaves and carries itself. The ultimate question we asked was, "Why does the lion behave this way?" The answer lies in its belief. Its belief system creates an attitude of confidence and authority.

Similarly, our belief systems shape our attitudes. When we are confident in our beliefs, we naturally develop an attitude that reflects this confidence and authority. Therefore, to cultivate a positive and empowering attitude, we must first examine and deal with our belief systems—our ideas, principles, and convictions.

## Belief and Attitude Connection:

Belief is the attitude that something is true or that something is the case. It is a mental acceptance of a fact, and this mental state of belief shapes our attitude.

**Defining Attitude:**

What is attitude? According to "yourdictionary.com," attitude is:

- A manner of thinking, feeling, or behaving that reflects a state of mind or disposition.

The state of your mind or disposition reflects what you think, and your thoughts create feelings, which in turn produce behaviors. Thus, another word for "your attitude" is **"your mindset."** Attitude is natural; it governs your behavior and actions. In fact, your attitude determines your future and the course of your life.

No wonder Winston Churchill famously said: "The empires of the future will be empires of the mind." - Winston Churchill (1943)

**The Power of Attitude:**

Your attitude determines the future you can accommodate in your mind, and the future you envision becomes the future you can have. Attitude defines everything. It opens doors of opportunity and creates new possibilities. Conversely, a negative or limiting attitude creates barriers and limitations, confining your potential.

In essence, your attitude is your life. It shapes your interactions, your responses to challenges, and the outcomes you experience. Understanding this deep connection between belief and attitude is the key to transforming your mindset and achieving the success and fulfillment you desire.

To cultivate a strong, positive attitude, focus on aligning your beliefs with empowering truths. Challenge limiting beliefs and replace them with thoughts that inspire confidence, resilience, and optimism. When your belief system is aligned with your goals and values, your attitude will naturally reflect a mindset that leads to success.

## Where Do Your Attitude Come From?

Your attitude originates from your beliefs. In other words, attitude is a direct product of belief. This implies that if attitude shapes the entire course of your life, and attitude stems from belief, then **your life is ultimately shaped by your belief system**. To achieve a positive outcome in life, you must address your belief system, which in turn will help create the right attitude towards life.

The incredible thing is that you can change the direction of your life simply by changing your attitude. Oprah Winfrey once said, and I wholeheartedly agree:

*"The greatest discovery of all time is that a person can change his future by merely changing his attitude." - Oprah Winfrey*

When I came to this realization, my life transformed completely. I was born in a small village in Africa, part of a family of 12 children. Both of my parents were illiterate and had no formal education—no primary, secondary, or tertiary schooling. There was no inherent motivation in my environment. My belief system was shaped by the circumstances of my immediate family and community.

To give you a sense of how poor we were: we only ate chicken in our house during festive seasons like Easter and Christmas. I have no memory of celebrating my birthday as a child. In fact, my first birthday celebration happened in my third year of university, when members of my Christian fellowship surprised me. My younger brother and I slept on a floor mat until I was about 15 years old.

What I'm trying to express is that my belief system led to low self-esteem. But when I gave my life to Christ and began reading the Bible, my beliefs began to shift. I started forming a new perspective of myself. As my belief system changed, my attitude towards life evolved as well. Today, by the grace of God, I have built my mother a beautiful home, worth thousands of dollars, among other accomplishments.

**How Did I Cultivate the Attitude That Led to My Success?**

Like Oprah said:

*"Step out of the history that is holding you back. Step into the new story you are willing to create." - Oprah Winfrey*

I stepped away from the history that shaped my limiting belief system and held me back. I began to see myself differently, to view myself as a success. I embraced the meaning of my name, "Nicholas," which means "the victory of the people." I started to see myself as the victory of my family, envisioning myself supporting orphans, providing for the destitute, and sponsoring students who were struggling. My attitude changed, and because my heart was set on being the victory for others, God placed the means in my hands to fulfill that mission. Hallelujah! To God be the glory.

I've also discovered that the key difference between a leader and a follower is **attitude**. Your attitude determines whether you will lead or follow. If your desire is to be a leader, then you must cultivate the attitude that reflects leadership—and this will naturally emerge from your belief system.

Always remember: **belief is the attitude that something is the case or true**. Change your belief, and you change your attitude. Change your attitude, and you change your life.


## The Power of Your Mindset

"You have the Creator's mental capacity. The mind you possess can shape your life and fill your emptiness with treasures. It can overcome and destroy all forms of darkness. This demonstrates the caliber of mind that a redeemed person possesses. You have what it takes to make things happen, so you cannot be stranded."

Perhaps it was the ancient Chinese philosopher Lao Tzu, who, more than 2,500 years ago, first wrote about the power of the mindset with these words:

*"Our mindset impacts the conscious, subconscious, and unconscious. It affects the way we think, our opinions, and the beliefs we form. Therefore, to have dominion over our lives, we must be intentional about protecting our mindset. When we are determined to improve, our newly empowered mindset will begin producing more driven thoughts. These thoughts, in turn, generate positive words, affirmative actions, and habits that sharpen our character and propel our destiny forward."*

Be mindful of how you think because your thoughts have powerful consequences.

Proverbs 4:23 emphasizes this truth:

*"Keep thy heart with all diligence; for out of it are the issues of life."* (AKJV)

*"Guard your heart above all else, for it determines the course of your life."* (NLT)

This wisdom is echoed by Ralph Waldo Emerson, who once said: *"Sow a thought and you reap an action; sow an act and you reap a habit; sow a habit and you reap a character; sow a character and you reap a destiny."*

Perhaps you, the reader of this book today, might finish reading and then set it aside, forgetting everything you've encountered within its pages. If that happens, you will remain exactly the same person, experiencing no change, growth or transformation. This would be because you haven't truly absorbed or internalized what I've shared with you.

# Chapter 6

# HOW DO WE FORM OR CREATE OUR BELIEF-SYSTEM?

As we have already established from the preceding chapters, belief systems have the power to dictate the direction and outcome of our lives, either for good or bad. But how do we form or create our belief systems? It is particularly important to understand how our belief systems are formed or created because it will help us in the process of reframing or reprogramming them.

Our beliefs are developed from childhood and often stick with us into adulthood. The truth is, from the very day we are born, our parents, culture, and environment heavily influence our thinking and beliefs. From my studies and research, I have come to the conclusion that the first seven years of our lives are the most crucial. During these early years, the groundwork for our perception of the world is laid. We start perceiving or apprehending by means of the senses or of the mind, building the foundation of our belief system. It is therefore crucial that we are fed positive belief systems that will eventually help us develop the right attitude in life.

The challenge, however, lies in the fact that we do not have control over the factors that shape us during these first formative years—factors such as parents, culture, environment, etc. This is the sad truth. Nonetheless, after these first seven years, our subconscious minds begin to be reprogrammed by life experiences. These experiences come through things people say to us, things we hear on the news, things we read, or any other external influences to which we are exposed.

Consequently, our past experiences and early childhood situations influence how we think about ourselves and others, and how we make sense of the world in our present state. Whether we like it or not, these experiences shape our core belief system. This belief system, in turn, influences our perceptions, emotions, values, habits, and reactions to life, ultimately determining the outcome of our lives. It is important to recognize that beliefs do not exist in isolation; they interact with one another, affecting each other and together forming a system.

In conclusion, we continuously form or create our belief systems every day for the rest of our lives. However, these belief systems evolve as part of our development throughout life—to ensure our survival as human beings.

## The Two Kinds of Belief: Information-Based & Faith-Based

In exploring how our belief systems are formed, it is essential to recognize that belief systems generally emerge from two sources of data: Information-Based Beliefs and Faith-Based Beliefs. Understanding the difference between these two kinds of beliefs can help us navigate how we form and adjust our beliefs over time.

## 1. Information-Based Beliefs

Information-based beliefs are rooted in knowledge or facts learned about a specific subject or event. These beliefs are formed when we believe something to be true because the available evidence suggests it is true.

One notable feature of information-based beliefs is that they are relatively easy to change. When presented with new information that contradicts our current beliefs, we are likely to adjust our beliefs accordingly. This makes information-based beliefs fluid, allowing them to evolve with the introduction of new data.

For example, if someone does not believe in the existence of dinosaurs due to a lack of information, that belief can change once they are presented with fossil evidence and scientific studies. Thus, new evidence can prove previously held beliefs wrong and help us adopt more accurate perspectives.

In summary, information-based beliefs are built on evidence and facts, making them susceptible to change when new information becomes available.

## 2. Faith-Based Beliefs

Faith-based beliefs are personal and internal. They are not dependent on external proof or evidence but are instead rooted in one's inner convictions, feelings, and experiences. These beliefs are much more resistant to change because they are shaped by personal belief rather than objective data.

Faith-based beliefs do not require validation from others, and they remain stable over time because they are founded on personal values and emotions. However, while faith-based beliefs are harder to change, they still influence the way we perceive the world around us.

Interestingly, there is a relationship between information-based beliefs and faith-based beliefs. For example, we may have faith that the information we possess is correct, leading us to trust in the accuracy of our information-based beliefs. Yet, as with faith-based beliefs, there is always the possibility that our faith in this information could be misplaced, and our beliefs could be proven wrong.

## Can Faith-Based Beliefs Be Proven Wrong?

This question is complex and multifaceted. On a universal level, faith-based beliefs are difficult to disprove because they do not rely on external evidence. However, on a personal level, faith-based beliefs can be challenged and transformed.

Rather than receiving new information that contradicts faith-based beliefs, a person may encounter a new perspective—a different way of seeing things—that reshapes their previously held beliefs. While this may not prove their beliefs wrong in an absolute sense, it may lead them to realize that those beliefs no longer serve them.

Moreover, sometimes information-based beliefs transform into faith-based beliefs. For example, despite extensive evidence for the existence of dinosaurs, some individuals choose not to believe in them. In such cases, their belief is based on personal faith rather than evidence. While their belief may not be wrong for them, it may conflict with the beliefs of those who accept the scientific evidence.

In conclusion, faith-based beliefs are more deeply ingrained and resistant to change than information-based beliefs, but both types of belief play essential roles in shaping our perception of the world and our place within it.

# Chapter 7

# BELIEFS & FAITH

In Chapter 2, we discussed that the word "belief" in Greek is "Pistis," which means "confidence" or "trust." This is the same word used for "faith" in Greek. Therefore, in the Bible, belief is often translated as faith—faith means belief.

Jesus speaks of this in Matthew 9:29:

*"Then He touched their eyes, saying, 'According to your faith let it be to you.'" (NKJV)*

The Greek word translated as "faith" here is "Pistis." According to Thayer's Greek-English Lexicon, it means *"conviction of the truth of anything,"* or *"belief with the predominant idea of trust (or confidence), whether in God or in Christ, springing from faith in the same."*

Jesus said, *"According to your faith."* Notice, He did not say "according to your education" or "according to your intelligence." It is always according to your faith. This is why education is not equal to a miracle, and intelligence does not result in a miracle. Miracles happen according to your faith—what you believe. Therefore, you are always a product of your beliefs.

Your life, at this very moment, is shaped by your belief system. The outcome of your life is a direct result of the contents of your beliefs. This is the message Jesus conveyed when He healed the two blind men in this passage. Their healing occurred because of their belief system—they believed that Jesus could heal them, and thus, they received their healing.

If you do not believe, you cannot become. It doesn't matter how educated or intelligent you are. As it's often said, "If you believe you can, you can. If you believe you can't, you can't." This is a universal truth: everything hinges on your belief.

However, you cannot fake belief. Your belief system will always reveal itself. This is a principle. Someone may make a positive confession, saying, "I am blessed," but their reality shows they are struggling financially. Similarly, someone may declare, "I am healed," but in truth, they are still ill. Why is this? It's because their belief system contradicts their confession.

What am I saying? Many confuse presumption with faith. Presumption is belief based on reasonable grounds or probable evidence. Faith, on the other hand, is belief beyond reasonable doubt—belief in credible evidence, even when it is not yet visible. Presumption is an assumption that something is true, while faith is an unwavering conviction that something is true. Presumption operates on probability, but faith leaves no room for doubt. With faith, you possess the evidence internally, even if you haven't yet seen the external results. This is why you cannot fake belief.

You cannot believe beyond your belief system. You can only believe within the limits of your belief system.

## True Faith - Confident Attitude Toward God

Let's take a deeper look at what it means to have a confident attitude toward God. Developing this confidence is foundational to living out a life of true faith, not just presumption.

Imagine airplanes taking off every day. Passengers trust a stranger to take them 32,000 feet into the air, confident that they will land safely. Yet, while standing on the ground, they might say, "I believe I would survive if I flew on an airplane." Is this belief or something else?

Many people "believe" in Jesus Christ in a similar way. They acknowledge His existence and His identity as God and Savior of the world, yet this is merely mental assent. It's an acknowledgment of facts. In James 2:19, even the demons are said to believe in this way.

But biblical faith goes beyond simply acknowledging the facts. Biblical faith is like actually buying a plane ticket, boarding the aircraft, fastening your seatbelt, and trusting the pilot to carry you safely to your destination. This is what it means to trust Jesus with your eternal destiny.

In John 5:24, Jesus said:

*"Truly, truly, I say to you, he who hears My word and believes Him who sent Me has eternal life and does not come into judgment but has passed out of death into life."*

This belief goes beyond acknowledgment—it is a complete trust in Jesus Christ with one's eternal destiny. The New Testament mentions "eternal life" more than 60 times, and it is always promised to those who put their faith—meaning their trust—entirely in Christ for salvation.

So, the real question is: Do you merely accept the facts as true, or are you truly trusting Christ with your eternal destiny?


## Faith and Belief: Two Sides of the Same Coin

Faith and belief are often used interchangeably, but they both represent a deep trust and confidence in God. Nelson's Bible Dictionary defines faith as "a belief in or confident attitude toward God, involving a commitment to His will for one's life." Belief, on the other hand, is defined as "placing one's trust in God's truth." In both cases, the emphasis is on trust and commitment.

Faith and belief are like the two rails of a train track—both are necessary for the train to safely reach its destination.

Though you may not be able to see faith or belief, like electricity, they are powerful forces that influence every aspect of your life.

The Greek word for faith, pisteuo, means persuasion or conviction. Its root, peitho, means to convince. Similarly, the Greek word for belief, pistis, means confidence or trust. Whether you are exercising faith or belief, you are ultimately expressing conviction based on the facts you hold to be true. As we go through life, we act on these convictions, whether they are based on our upbringing, education, or personal experiences with God.

Hebrews 11:1 provides the most profound definition of faith:

*"Now faith is the assurance of things hoped for, the conviction of things not seen."*

Faith and belief are interconnected. They are the internal forces that guide us as we trust God and follow His direction, even when the results are not yet visible.

# Chapter 8

# BELIEFS & PHILOSOPHY

Philosophy is a product of ideas. But what is Philosophy?

The ancient Greek word for philosophy is "philosophia," which literally means "love of wisdom" or "friend of wisdom." According to Wikipedia, Philosophy is the study of general and fundamental questions about existence, knowledge, values, reason, mind, and language.

Philosophy is a compound word. If split into two, we get: "philo" and "osophy."

- "Philo" means to love.
- "Osophy" means a belief or doctrine, an "ism."

This is interesting. As we have already established, belief is the mental acceptance of, and conviction in, the truth, actuality, or validity of something. Philosophy, therefore, has to do with mental reasoning. So, **philosophy means to think about your thoughts until you believe them**. In essence, your philosophy is your belief system. Your belief system stems from your ideas. When you dwell on your ideas until they become convictions, you are inevitably creating your belief system.

Therefore, your belief system arises from a collection of ideas you have accumulated over the years. To change your belief system, we must change your ideas—your philosophies. Do you know what I am doing to you right now as you are reading this book? I am attacking your ideas. Yes, I am challenging your old ideas.

## What is an Idea?

An idea is a thought, belief, opinion, or plan. In this context, permit me to say that ideas are thoughts that communicate belief. Books, messages, and sermons are simply collections of ideas. When you buy a book, you are purchasing a chest of ideas. When you read a book, you are collecting ideas, and those ideas have the power to challenge your old or existing ones. You will never change until you are exposed to a new idea.

This is why many people don't grow beyond their current state. They are constantly reinforcing the same ideas that originally shaped their belief system. For instance, if someone watches too much television—specifically, the same programs repeatedly—it infuses the same ideas that are contributing to their stagnant belief system. The television keeps repeating the same content, and if someone keeps consuming that content, they will gradually embody the ideas of the television, consciously or not.

Proverbs 23:7 (NKJV) says: "*For as he thinks in his heart, so is he. 'Eat and drink!' he says to you, but his heart is not with you.*"

This verse is often misquoted as: *"As a man thinketh, so is he."* But the Bible doesn't say that. The correct phrase is: *"As a man thinks in his heart, so is he."* The emphasis is on *"in his heart."* By implication, the thinking is done in the heart. What you think in your heart, you become. This verse revolutionized my life—it transported me from my past self into the person I am today. It transformed me from a boy with a poor background into a life of success and prosperity.

You don't change until the contents of your heart change. And by the way, the *"heart"* mentioned in the Bible isn't the one in your chest; it refers to your mind. The word "heart" is used to symbolize the mind. For instance, when the Bible says in Luke 6:45 (NKJV): "*A good man out of the good treasure of his heart brings forth good; and an evil man out of the evil treasure of his heart brings forth evil. For out of the abundance of the heart his mouth speaks.*"

You will agree with me that your physical heart doesn't talk. This passage is referring to your mind. The Greek word translated "heart" in this verse is "kardia." According to Strong's Greek-English Lexicon, "kardia" means: "the thoughts or feelings (mind)." According to Thayer's Greek-English Lexicon, it means:

- "The soul or mind."
- "Of the understanding, the faculty and seat of the intelligence."
- "Of the will and character."

So, the word *"heart"* can be understood as *"sub-mind."* You have a conscious mind and a subconscious mind. Your conscious mind is what you are using to read this book right now. Your subconscious mind collects the things you decide to believe from what you are reading. You store what you believe in your subconscious mind, and that is where you live from.

Let's look at an illustration that treats the human mind as an information system (like a computer). If the *"heart"* is your hard drive, your subconscious mind is your desktop. The desktop only shows what you want others to see, while your hard drive contains everything—the real you. The hard drive determines what the computer can do or cannot do. Similarly, you are not defined by what you show; you are defined by what you have stored.

The real question becomes: *Where have you been getting your ideas from?* This is the ultimate question in changing your belief system. Initially, the hard drive of your mind is a blank slate, but over time, you download information into it. Whatever you download becomes your reality. The key to how this affects and drives your belief system will be discussed in the subsequent chapters.

# Chapter 9

# THE CONCEPT OF SPIRIT, SOUL & BODY

In this chapter, we will discuss the concept of man as a *triune being*, exploring the relationship between the spirit, soul, and body. It is essential to note that the word *man* here refers to all human beings, irrespective of gender. Understanding this relationship is key to comprehending the makeup of humans, their belief systems, and how this impacts their lives.

Man is a triune being, meaning he is a combination of three distinct yet interconnected parts: spirit, soul, and body. He is not merely a physical being, as often perceived. Man consists of these three parts, as highlighted by Paul in 1 Thessalonians 5:23 (KJV): *"And the very God of peace sanctify you **wholly**; and I pray God your whole **spirit and soul and body** be preserved blameless unto the coming of our Lord Jesus Christ."*

The word *wholly* in this context refers to the entirety or fullness of man—his complete and total being, which comprises spirit, soul, and body. This reinforces the notion that man is a composite of these three elements.

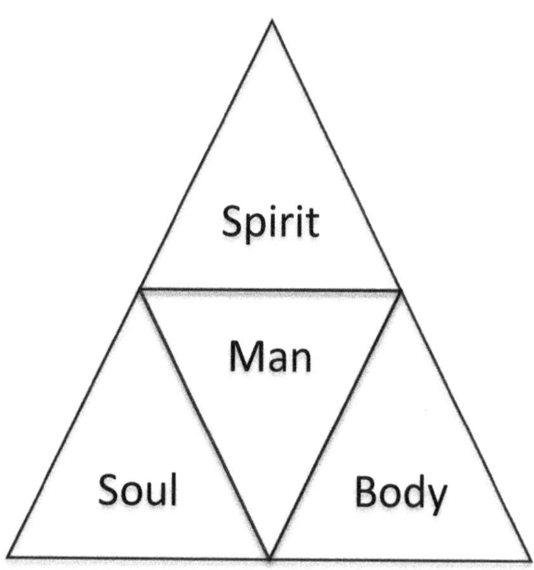


The Bible further clarifies this concept in Hebrews 4:12 (KJV): *"For the word of God is quick, and powerful, and sharper than any twoedged sword, piercing even to the dividing asunder of soul and spirit, and of the joints and marrow, and is a discerner of the thoughts and intents of the heart."*

In this verse, the Bible draws a distinction between the soul and spirit, as well as between joints and marrow, which clearly refers to the body. When read in the Amplified Bible (AMP), the verse states: *"For the word of God is living and active and full of power [making it operative, energizing, and effective]. It is sharper than any two-edged sword, penetrating as far as the division of the soul and spirit [the completeness of a person], and of both joints and marrow [the deepest parts of our nature], exposing and judging the very thoughts and intentions of the heart."*

This passage illustrates that the three parts of a person—spirit, soul, and body—are separate yet integrally linked. From this understanding, we conclude that man is first and foremost a *spirit being*, possessing a soul and inhabiting a body.

Many people, however, do not fully comprehend this spiritual reality. As a result, they often experience issues such as setbacks, depression, anxiety, and fear, which can be traced back to a lack of understanding of the relationship between spirit, soul, and body. These problems are rooted in their belief systems.

A failure to grasp the distinctions and interconnections between the spirit, soul, and body can have profound consequences on one's attitude, emotions, behavior, and reactions to life's challenges—ultimately affecting the outcome of their lives.

This is a crucial concept to understand, as it sheds light on how deeply intertwined our spiritual, emotional, and physical health is with our belief systems. Understanding this relationship enables us to navigate life with greater clarity, aligning our actions with our spiritual essence to live in harmony with God's design for us.

The relationship between the spirit, soul, and body is fundamental to understanding how humans operate on different levels—spiritually, mentally, emotionally, and physically. Let's delve deeper into each aspect:

**The Spirit**

- **God-Consciousness:** The spirit is the part of man that connects and communicates with God. Through the spirit, we are able to engage with the spiritual realm and maintain a relationship with our Creator. The spirit influences both the soul and the body.
- **The Real Man:** The spirit is the core essence of a person. It has the power to inspire and guide the soul and body. It is what gives man his identity.
- **Made up of Intuition, Conscience, and Communion:** These three components form the structure of the spirit:
  - **Intuition:** The ability to perceive truth and gain spiritual knowledge without relying on reasoning.
  - **Conscience:** The inner sense of right and wrong, which guides moral decisions.
  - **Communion:** The ability to communicate and connect with God through worship, prayer, and fellowship.

## The Soul

- **Self-Consciousness:** The soul is responsible for man's interaction with other people. It is the center of emotions, thoughts, and decisions, acting as the psychological engine that powers our mental and emotional processes.
- **Link Between Spirit and Body:** The soul acts as the intermediary between the spirit and the body. It receives input from the body and passes it to the spirit, and vice versa. It interprets and transmits spiritual truths to the body and material realities to the spirit.
- **Made up of Mind, Will, and Emotion:**
    - **Mind (Thinker):** The intellectual aspect of the soul that processes information, makes decisions, and forms beliefs.
    - **Will (Chooser):** The part that exercises choice and determines actions.
    - **Emotion (Feeler):** The center of feelings and emotional experiences that shape responses to life's events.

## The Body

- **World-Consciousness:** The body is the part of man that engages with the physical world through the senses. It is the physical structure that houses the spirit and soul, and it enables interaction with the environment.

- **The Executioner of Thought:** The body carries out the instructions of the spirit and soul. Whatever the spirit and soul contemplate, the body performs.
- **Made up of the Five Senses:**
  - **Sight, Hearing, Taste, Touch, Smell:** These senses allow man to perceive and engage with the physical world. They provide information to the soul, which then processes it and responds.

## The Interaction Between Spirit, Soul, and Body

- The **spirit** speaks to the **soul**, inspiring and guiding it. The **soul**, in turn, takes what it has received from the **spirit** and relays it to the **body**. Conversely, the **body** takes in information from the physical world through the five senses and sends this data to the **soul**, which interprets and communicates it to the **spirit**.
- The **soul** is the mediator, regulating and controlling what flows between the **spirit** and **body**. It ensures the connection between the divine (spirit) and the material (body), maintaining harmony between them.

## Diagram Overview

The diagram below would illustrate the flow of communication and influence between the three parts. The **spirit** would be at the top, symbolizing its higher connection to God and its influence over the soul. The **soul** would be in the middle, mediating between the **spirit** and

**body.** The **body** would be at the bottom, representing the physical and earthly realm, receiving instructions from the soul.

The flow of information would move both ways—vertically—from **body** to **soul** to **spirit**, and vice versa. The key takeaway is that man's total experience is the result of an ongoing interaction between these three elements. This relationship plays a significant role in determining a person's health, attitude, behavior, and overall quality of life.

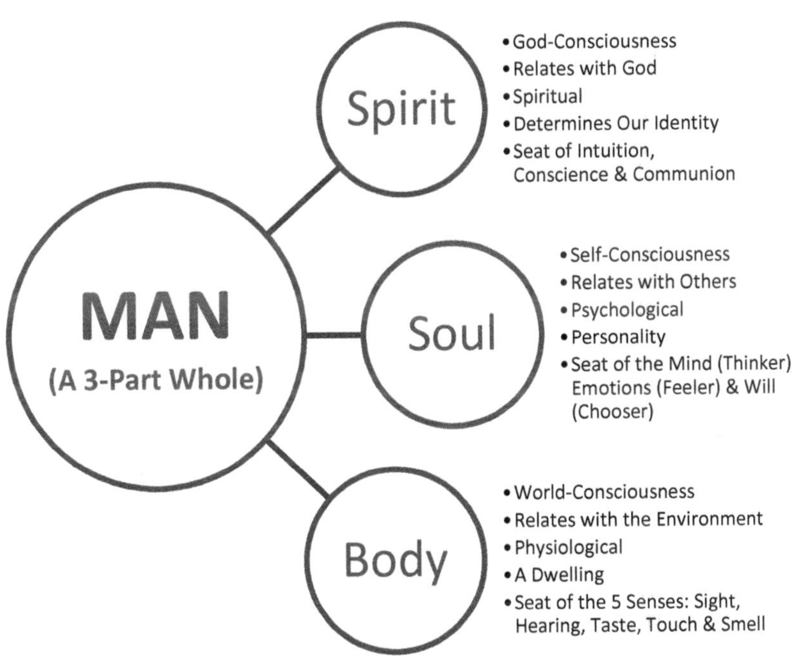

## The Workings of the Spirit, the Soul, and the Body

The interaction between the spirit, soul, and body in humans is a sophisticated process that reflects the harmonious relationship among these three components, leading to actions and results. Here's a more detailed breakdown of this process:

### 1. The Body Receives Information

- The body, through its five senses—**sight, hearing, taste, touch, and smell**—is responsible for receiving external information from the physical world. This could be anything from a sound or a smell to physical sensations or visual stimuli.
- This external input is the starting point for the entire process of perception, decision-making, and action.

### 2. The Body Transmits Information to the Soul

- Once the body receives the information, it quickly transmits it to the **soul**. The **soul** is responsible for processing these inputs at a psychological and emotional level.
- The **soul** acts as the central processing unit for the body and spirit. It examines the data received from the body and begins the process of determining how to react.

### 3. The Soul Processes the Information

- The **soul,** composed of the **mind (thinker), will (chooser),** and **emotions (feeler),** plays a critical role at this stage:
    - **Belief:** Before the soul fully processes the information, it first determines whether it believes the input. It must assess whether the information aligns with its existing belief system.
    - **Processing:** After belief is established, the soul begins to analyze the information. This involves thinking, reasoning, and considering past experiences, memories, and learned knowledge to interpret the input.
    - **Transmission to Spirit:** Once the soul has processed the information, it sends this data to the **spirit** for further consideration and direction.

## 4. The Spirit Receives and Conceives

- When the **spirit** receives the processed information from the soul, it plays a crucial role in providing **spiritual insight** and **discernment.** The spirit has a higher connection to **God-consciousness** and is thus capable of understanding spiritual truths that go beyond mere physical and emotional responses.
- The **spirit conceives** and **analyzes** the information. Through its **intuition, conscience,** and **communion,** the spirit interprets the data from a spiritual

perspective, giving deeper meaning or clarity that is rooted in divine understanding.

## 5. The Spirit Gives Direction

- After receiving and analyzing the information, the **spirit** issues instructions back to the **soul.** These instructions guide the soul on how to respond to the initial input from the body.
- The direction from the spirit aligns with the individual's spiritual beliefs, morals, and connection to God. It influences the decisions, choices, and emotions that the soul will transmit back to the body.

## 6. The Soul Instructs the Body

- Once the **soul** has received guidance from the **spirit**, it then directs the **body** on how to act or respond. The **soul,** as the intermediary, bridges the spiritual insights of the spirit with the physical actions of the body.
- This could result in various forms of action—speaking, moving, reacting emotionally, or making decisions based on the processed information.

## 7. The Body Executes the Action

- Finally, the **body** acts upon the instructions received from the soul, which were informed by the **spirit.** The body performs the necessary physical actions, such as moving, speaking, or responding to the environment.

**In Summary**

- **Input (Body):** The body collects information from the external world through the senses.
- **Processing (Soul):** The soul believes, processes, and interprets the data received from the body.
- **Direction (Spirit):** The spirit conceives the processed information and provides spiritual direction back to the soul.
- **Execution (Soul to Body):** The soul instructs the body on the appropriate response based on the direction from the spirit.
- **Action (Body):** The body executes the physical actions, completing the cycle.

This interconnection reflects how the **spirit, soul**, and **body** collaborate to produce outcomes in a person's life, shaped by both external experiences and internal spiritual guidance.

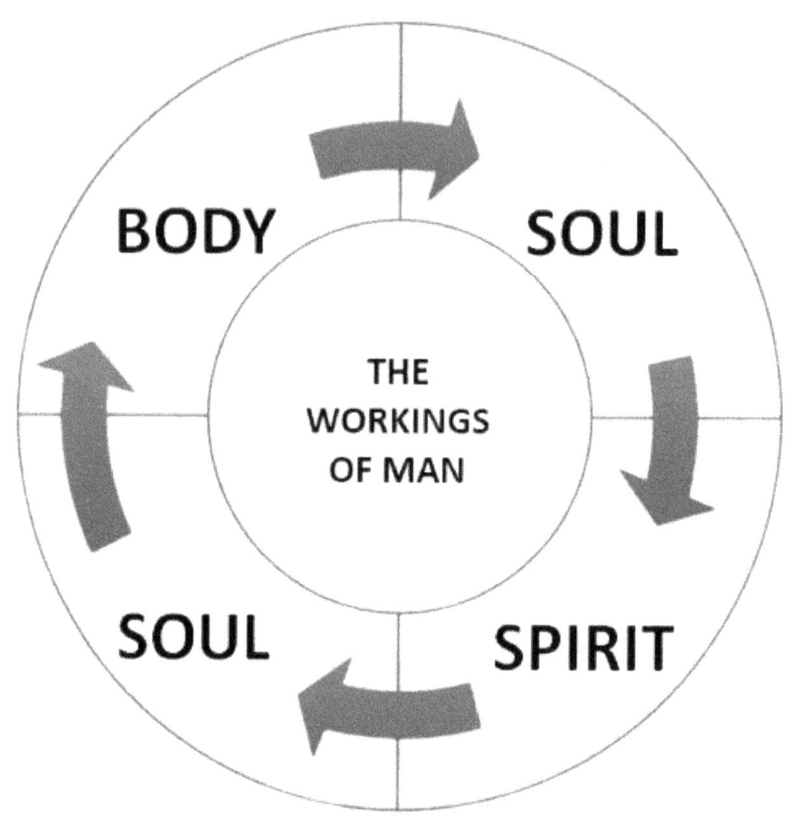



**The Battle of the Soul**

The battle of the soul arises from a conflict within the feedback loop between the spirit and the body, as the soul mediates between the two. As we have already established, the soul plays a critical role in transmitting information from the spirit to the body and vice versa. However, tension occurs when the body resists the spirit's direction, leading to a struggle within the soul as it attempts to reconcile the differences between the two. For example, your spirit may prompt the soul, saying, *"The information you received from the body is not in alignment with the truth."* Meanwhile, the soul responds, *"But this is what the body has given me."*

It is crucial to note that the soul cannot transmit to the spirit what it has not received from the body. The soul functions as a regulator and controller, determining what reaches the spirit and feeding back information from the spirit to the body. The soul only transmits what it has received. Thus, for the soul to change the content it delivers to the spirit, the body must first change its source of information. This is why the Bible emphasizes the importance of hearing the Word of God. Romans 10:17 (NKJV) states: *"So then faith comes by hearing, and hearing by the word of God."*

The input we receive directly influences the soul's output, which in turn affects the alignment between body and spirit. This concept will be explored further in subsequent chapters. For now, consider the following figure as a graphical representation of the relationship between the spirit, soul, and body.

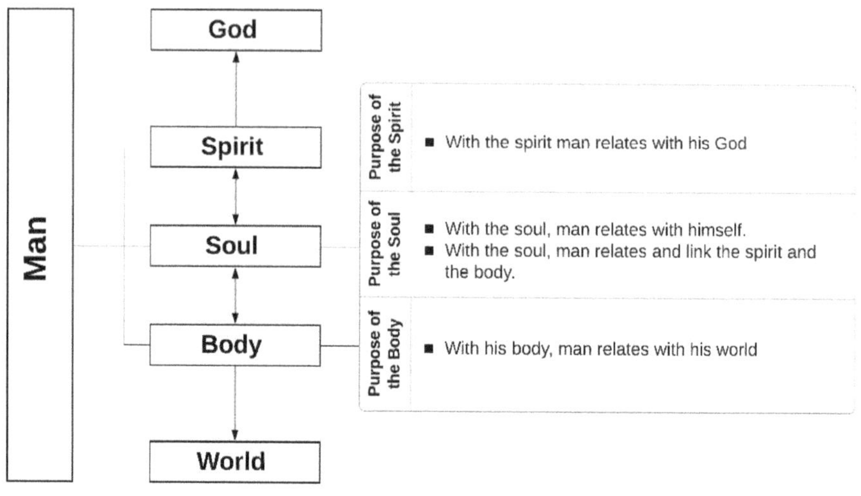


## The Battle in a "Born Again" Believer

The dynamics of the soul's battle shift significantly when an individual is "born again," or has a regenerated spirit. The Bible speaks to this transformation in 2 Corinthians 5:17 (NKJV): *"Therefore, if anyone is in Christ, he is a new creation; old things have passed away; behold, all things have become new."*

To be born again means to be in Christ—accepting Him as your Lord and Savior through the confession of sins and declaring Jesus as your Savior. The moment you do this, you become a new creation. In other words, your spirit becomes regenerated, and you receive the Spirit of God. With this regeneration, the feedback loop between the spirit and the body changes dramatically.

This transformation alters how the soul mediates between the body and spirit. Since the spirit is now aligned with God's truth, the soul begins receiving new instructions from the spirit, and the body is expected to follow suit. However, this doesn't always happen automatically. The body, with its old habits and desires, may still resist the spirit's influence, which leads to an ongoing battle within the soul.

In a regenerated believer, this battle often involves the soul's struggle to keep the body in check and in alignment with the directives of the regenerated spirit. The goal is to align the body's actions with the will of the spirit, which is now in harmony with God's will. The journey of a born-again believer involves continuous spiritual growth, the renewing of the mind, and overcoming the resistance of the flesh.

This transformation is profound, and the key to victory in this battle lies in the renewing of the mind and the submission of the body to the spirit. Through faith, discipline, and consistent feeding on the Word of God, the believer can bring the body into alignment with the regenerated spirit, and the soul can fulfill its purpose of ensuring harmony between the two.

**What Happens When the Man Has a Regenerated Spirit?**

When a person is born again and possesses a regenerated spirit, the spirit aligns itself with the demands and guidance of the Spirit of God. This alignment is due to the fact that the regenerated spirit is now attuned to God's truth and righteousness. Here's how the process works:

- **Alignment with God's Spirit:** The regenerated spirit conforms with the Spirit of God, desiring to live in harmony with God's will and commands. As the spirit is now in communion with God, it strives for righteousness and purity.
- **Conflict with Unjust Information:** If the body, through the soul, transmits any information that is unjust or out of alignment with God's truth, the regenerated spirit will immediately reject it. The spirit will say to the soul, *"The information you are transmitting from the body is not just. Tell the body to regulate or change the information."*
- **Submission of the Soul and Body:** Since the man now has a regenerated spirit, the soul and body are more inclined to accept the commands from the spirit. There is a greater willingness to adjust and align with the spirit's guidance because the soul has been influenced by the regenerated spirit. The body will either adjust its behavior or seek a new source of information that aligns with the spirit's demands.

## What Happens When the Man Does Not Have a Regenerated Spirit?

In contrast, when a person does not have a regenerated spirit, the process of aligning the body and soul with God's truth is much more challenging:

- **Resistance to the Spirit of God:** The spirit of an unregenerated man does not naturally conform to the demands of the Spirit of God. Since the man lacks the Spirit of God, his spirit is weak and prone to yielding to the desires and inclinations of the body.
- **Conflict with Unjust Information:** When the unregenerated spirit receives unjust information from the body through the soul, it may still recognize that something is wrong. However, the soul and body, being in a state of spiritual weakness, may resist the spirit's guidance. The soul may begin to contemplate the feedback from the spirit but finds itself in a state of inner conflict.
- **The Battle of the Soul:** The soul finds itself in a battle between the spirit's warning and the body's desires. The spirit urges the soul to regulate or change the information, but the body resists, insisting, *"I like how it feels."* This ongoing struggle creates a feedback loop of disagreement and resistance.
- **Pressure from the Body:** The body continues to pressure the soul, urging it to indulge in the physical and emotional

sensations it finds pleasurable, even though the soul knows it is wrong. The body says to the soul, *"Come on, feel it,"* and when the soul indulges in the body's desires, it feeds this information back to the spirit.

- **Yielding to the Body:** Because the man's spirit is not regenerated and lacks the strength of the Spirit of God, the soul eventually gives in to the body's desires. The spirit, lacking power, downloads the junk transmitted from the body through the soul. This yielding leads to a host of negative outcomes in the person's life, such as depression, anxiety, fear, setbacks, and a lack of spiritual peace.

## The Role of the Soul

From this outline, it becomes clear that the soul plays a critical and pivotal role in the workings of the spirit, soul, and body. The soul acts as the mediator between the body and the spirit, deciding whether to accept or reject the information received from the body. It is the soul that regulates what the body hears, sees, feels, smells, and tastes, and how it reacts to its environment.

For the person with a regenerated spirit, the soul is more aligned with the spirit's demands and guidance, making it easier to reject the body's negative inclinations. But for the person without a regenerated spirit, the soul struggles to resist the body's desires, leading to a cycle of spiritual defeat and frustration.

Thus, the regeneration of the spirit is crucial for the soul to function effectively in aligning the body with God's will and maintaining spiritual well-being.

## The Battle of the Soul

The battle of the soul intensifies when there is a conflict between the desires and information that the body transmits and the spiritual direction that the regenerated spirit provides. This battle is especially pronounced in individuals who have been "born again" and now possess a renewed spirit. As we delve deeper into this dynamic, we see how the soul is caught in the tension between the physical body, which often acts based on worldly stimuli and desires, and the spirit, which receives direction from God and seeks to lead the individual in alignment with divine truth.

## The Conflict Between the Body and the Spirit

When a person is born again, their spirit is renewed and regenerated by the Holy Spirit. This newly reborn spirit is inclined towards God's will, desiring to follow the Word of God and live in obedience to Him. The **spirit** is now in tune with divine truth, receiving direction from God and pushing the person towards righteousness, purity, and spiritual growth.

On the other hand, the **body**—still rooted in the physical world and subject to its natural desires and influences—

continues to send information to the **soul** based on worldly experiences, senses, and emotions. The body may crave things that are not in line with God's will, such as sinful habits, indulgences, or distractions that keep the person from living a spiritual life.

## The Soul's Role in the Battle

The soul acts as a mediator between the body and the spirit. It processes the desires, thoughts, and feelings coming from both the body and the spirit and attempts to make sense of them. However, when the body and spirit are in conflict—when the body desires something that the spirit knows is wrong—the **soul** experiences tension.

In this battle, the **soul** must decide which direction to take; either to follow the impulses of the body or to align with the guidance of the spirit. This decision can be difficult, especially if the soul is accustomed to following the body's desires. This conflict often results in internal struggles, emotional turmoil, and feelings of guilt, frustration, or doubt.

## How the Soul Overcomes the Battle

The key to overcoming the battle of the soul is in aligning the soul more closely with the spirit, which is in harmony with God's will. The Bible provides wisdom and guidance on how to strengthen the soul so that it follows the spirit rather than the body. Here are several principles that help in this alignment:

1. **Renewing the Mind with God's Word:**

   The Bible speaks of the importance of renewing the mind: *"Do not be conformed to this world, but be transformed by the renewing of your mind, that you may prove what is that good and acceptable and perfect will of God."* - Romans 12:2 (NKJV). The soul must constantly be fed with the Word of God so that its thoughts, emotions, and decisions align with the spirit rather than the flesh. The more the soul is exposed to God's truth, the less it will be influenced by the world's lies.

2. **Walking by the Spirit:**

   The Bible encourages believers to walk by the Spirit, meaning to live in accordance with the Holy Spirit's guidance: *"Walk in the Spirit, and you shall not fulfill the lust of the flesh."* - Galatians 5:16 (NKJV). When the soul allows the spirit to lead, rather than being driven by the body, the believer will experience victory over fleshly desires and temptations.

3. **Filling the Soul with Faith:**

   As noted in Romans 10:17, *"faith comes by hearing, and hearing by the word of God."* The soul needs to be constantly nourished with God's Word, which builds faith. Faith empowers the soul to trust in God's promises and to make decisions based on spiritual truth rather than physical desires.

4. **Crucifying the Flesh:**

The Bible speaks about crucifying the flesh, which means denying the body's sinful desires and submitting to the spirit's guidance: *"And those who are Christ's have crucified the flesh with its passions and desires."* - Galatians 5:24 (NKJV). The more the soul cooperates with the spirit in resisting the flesh, the less influence the body will have over the soul.

5.  **Seeking God's Strength:**
    Prayer and dependence on God's strength are crucial for overcoming the battle of the soul. By seeking God's help, the believer can be empowered to resist the flesh and follow the spirit's lead.

## Conclusion: Victory in the Battle

The battle of the soul is a daily struggle for believers, but victory is assured when the soul aligns with the spirit, which is guided by the Holy Spirit and God's Word. By continually renewing the mind, walking by the Spirit, and crucifying the flesh, the believer can experience freedom from the power of the body and live a life that pleases God.

Ultimately, the battle of the soul reflects the ongoing sanctification process, where the believer is continually being made more like Christ as the spirit gains greater control over the soul and body. Through this process, the believer grows in faith, maturity, and spiritual power.

In understanding what happens when a man has or does not have a regenerated spirit, we see that the soul plays a pivotal role in mediating between the body and the spirit. Here is a deeper look at the implications:

**When the Man Has a Regenerated Spirit:**

1. **Conformity with God's Spirit:**
   When the man's spirit is regenerated, it is in alignment with the Holy Spirit. The regenerated spirit is sensitive to God's direction, truth, and righteousness. The spirit will immediately discern anything that is unjust or contrary to God's will, coming from the body through the soul.

2. **Prompt Correction:**
   Upon receiving unjust information from the body, the regenerated spirit will reject it and command the soul to instruct the body to change its input. For instance, if the body experiences temptation or indulges in something sinful, the spirit will reject it and direct the soul to correct the body's actions or desires.

3. **Soul and Body's Compliance:**
   Because the man has a regenerated spirit, the soul and body are more likely to be submissive to the spirit's direction. The Holy Spirit empowers the man to overcome temptations of the flesh, so the body will adjust or regulate the information it receives. The soul, being in alignment with the spirit, cooperates by

reinforcing godly behaviors and rejecting worldly influences.

**When the Man Does Not Have a Regenerated Spirit:**

1. **Disconnection from God's Spirit:**

   In this state, the man's spirit is not in alignment with the Holy Spirit. Though the spirit can still discern right from wrong to some extent, it lacks the power and conviction of the Holy Spirit to resist the body's demands. The spirit is left without divine strength to overcome the temptations and desires of the flesh.

2. **Conflict and Resistance:**

   Even though the spirit may disagree with the unjust information received from the body, the body's desires are often stronger. When the soul attempts to correct the body, it encounters resistance because the body prioritizes immediate gratification and the "feel-good" emotions over righteousness.

3. **The Soul's Struggle:**

   The soul, caught in the middle of this tug-of-war, faces the "battle of the soul." The body continues to exert pressure, convincing the soul that its desires are worth indulging in. The soul may feel conflicted, knowing something is wrong, but unable to overcome the influence of the body because the spirit lacks the empowerment of God's presence.

4. **Submission to the Flesh:**
   Without the regenerated spirit, the soul often caves to the body's influence. Over time, the body's desires override the spirit's weakened objections. This lack of spiritual regeneration leads to various negative consequences like depression, anxiety, fear, and ongoing sin because the body, unchecked, governs the man's actions.

## The Role of the Soul:

- The soul, acting as a mediator, must navigate between the desires of the body and the discernment of the spirit. Its position makes it the key player in determining whether a man's life is led by the Spirit or by the flesh.
- **In the Regenerated Man**, the soul reinforces the guidance of the spirit because it has the divine backing of the Holy Spirit. It is empowered to resist the body's impulses, keeping the person aligned with God's will.
- **In the Unregenerated Man**, the soul struggles to resist the body because it lacks the spiritual strength provided by the Holy Spirit. Consequently, the soul may succumb to the body's sinful desires, leading to emotional and spiritual unrest.

Understanding the dynamics between the spirit, soul, and body reveals that the regeneration of the spirit is crucial for living a victorious and spiritually healthy life. When the spirit is regenerated and empowered by the Holy Spirit, it strengthens the soul to keep the body in check, aligning the person's life with God's will. Without this regeneration, the soul often succumbs to the body's desires, leading to a life ruled by the flesh rather than the spirit.

This interplay underscores the importance of spiritual renewal, sanctification, and ongoing submission to God's Spirit for those seeking to live a life of spiritual victory and peace.

# Chapter 10

# THE CONCEPT OF THE MIND

The mind is understood in various ways across different cultures and religious traditions. Despite this diversity, it is generally accepted that the mind is what enables a being to have subjective awareness, intentionality, and the ability to perceive and respond to their environment. It is also the seat of consciousness, encompassing thoughts and emotions.

At its core, the mind is the element that allows a person to be aware of the world, to experience it, to think about it, and to feel emotions related to it. In essence, it is the faculty of consciousness and thought. The mind comprises both cognitive and non-cognitive aspects, each contributing to how we perceive reality and how we respond to stimuli.

To fully grasp the concept of the mind, it is essential to explore its various aspects, which include cognition, emotions, and deeper subconscious processes. These components work together to shape our experiences, thoughts, and interactions with the world around us.

**Aspects of the Mind**

The mind can be divided into two primary aspects:

1.  **Cognitive Aspect**

    This aspect refers to the mental action or processes involved in acquiring knowledge and understanding through thought, experience, and the senses. In simpler terms, cognition is the mental process of thinking and understanding, along with the insights that arise from this process. For instance, when you learn how to solve a new math problem, you are engaging your cognitive faculties.

    The cognitive aspects of the mind include:

    - **Perception:** How we interpret sensory information.
    - **Recognition:** The ability to identify previously encountered information or patterns.
    - **Conception:** Forming ideas and abstract thinking.
    - **Judgment:** Evaluating information to make decisions.
    - **Reasoning:** Logical thinking and problem-solving.
    - **Imagination:** Creating mental images and concepts not present to the senses.
    - **Intuition:** Understanding something instinctively, without the need for conscious reasoning.
    - **Language:** The ability to use words to communicate ideas.

- **Memory:** Storing and retrieving information.
- **Consciousness:** Awareness of one's existence and environment.

Cognitive processes are vital for using existing knowledge and generating new insights, making them essential for learning and adaptation.

2. **Non-Cognitive Aspect**

This aspect of the mind refers to processes not directly related to conscious intellectual activity. Non-cognitive factors influence motivation, integrity, interpersonal interactions, and emotional responses. While they may indirectly involve intellectual activity, they are more related to feelings, personality, and temperament.

The non-cognitive aspects of the mind include:

- **Emotions:** Feelings that influence behavior and decision-making.
- **Personality:** An individual's characteristic patterns of thinking, feeling, and behaving.
- **Temperament:** The basic emotional and behavioral traits that are biologically influenced.
- **Attitudes:** The learned tendency to evaluate things in a certain way, which can be shaped by beliefs and experiences.

## Key Differentiations

- **The Mind vs. The Brain:** The brain is a physical organ, a tangible part of our body located in our skull. The mind, however, is non-physical, representing consciousness and awareness. It is not confined to a specific location like the brain. The mind processes and generates thoughts, ideas, and experiences, while the brain is the physical structure that enables these processes.

- **The Mind vs. Thoughts:** Thoughts are specific mental activities or processes, like internal conversations we have with ourselves. Thoughts are part of the broader concept of the mind, which encompasses all mental activities, including emotions, perceptions, and memories. Thought is just one of many mental faculties that the mind can engage in.

## The Power of the Human Mind

A key characteristic of the mind is its privacy. No one else can access or fully know your mind but you. Others may interpret your words, actions, or body language, but the true contents of your mind—your thoughts, emotions, and ideas—are entirely private. This privacy gives the mind immense power, as it holds the keys to our inner world, shaping our reality, behavior, and how we interact with the external world.

## Classification of the Mind

The human mind is typically divided into two main parts: the "Conscious Mind" and the "Unconscious Mind." Sandwiched between these two is the "Subconscious Mind," which remains in continuous contact with the unconscious mind. Due to this close connection, many scholars consider the subconscious mind as part of the unconscious mind, choosing not to distinguish them. For the purpose of this book, this perspective will shape our understanding of how the belief system operates.

However, in terms of our levels of awareness, Sigmund Freud, the renowned Austrian psychologist, who is perhaps best known for popularizing the concept of the human mind having distinct levels, classified the mind into three broad and distinct parts:

- Conscious Mind
- Subconscious (Preconscious) Mind
- Unconscious Mind

These three parts of the mind work together, yet each has its own unique role in shaping our thoughts, actions, and beliefs.

## 1. The Conscious Mind

The conscious mind is the first of the three levels of awareness. It encompasses everything we are aware of at any given moment. This includes what you are currently thinking about, both externally and internally. For example, you are aware of your environment, breathing, and the people around you. If you are aware of it, then it exists within your conscious mind.

Right now, as you are reading this book, you may also be thinking, "This book is quite good. I will recommend it to my friends." Both of these thoughts are occurring in your conscious mind, which handles your present, moment-to-moment awareness.

## 2. The Subconscious (Preconscious) Mind

The subconscious mind, also known as the preconscious, is the second level of awareness. It consists of information just beneath the surface of our conscious awareness, which can be easily retrieved with a little focus. This part of the mind acts like a vast memory bank, storing accessible information, such as memories, habits, and skills.

We are not always consciously aware of the stored information in the subconscious mind until we direct our attention to it, a process known as "memory recall." For example, driving home from work without consciously thinking about the route, or walking down a familiar street without needing to be alert, are both instances where the subconscious mind is in action. You know the path home, but you aren't actively thinking about it until something in your surrounding grabs or captures your attention.

To simplify: **Subconscious Mind = Stored Information + Memories of Life**

A clear example of using your subconscious mind is remembering frequently dialed phone numbers without effort. Similarly, after years of driving experience, you can drive a car almost automatically, as your subconscious mind manages the actions, like shifting gears and turning the steering wheel.

## 3. The Unconscious Mind

The unconscious mind is the deepest of the three levels of awareness. It stores thoughts, memories, and desires that are buried well below the conscious level, exerting significant influence on our behavior without us being aware of them.

In this context, "unconscious" refers not to being physically unconscious but to deeply ingrained beliefs and ideas that affect our lives without our knowledge. It encompasses reactions, instinctive behavior, and personality traits that are often shaped by past experiences, even if we can't consciously remember them.

The unconscious mind holds countless memories and experiences we've accumulated throughout our lifetime. We can't readily access these stored memories or thoughts on demand. For example, traumatic experiences or long-buried memories from childhood are stored here. These unconscious memories typically don't surface easily, but under certain conditions, they can move into the subconscious mind and sometimes even into conscious awareness, such as when a long-forgotten memory suddenly comes back to us.

However, retrieving unconscious memories often requires a strong trigger, whereas memories stored in the subconscious are more easily brought to the surface of consciousness.

# Chapter 11

# THE POWER OF THE SUBCONSCIOUS MIND & ITS ROLE IN BELIEF SYSTEMS

Many scholars argue that the subconscious mind is the most powerful among the three levels of the mind—conscious, subconscious, and unconscious. This notion is crucial in understanding the belief systems discussed in this book because the subconscious mind directly influences the unconscious mind, the storehouse of all memories and past experiences. Since beliefs, habits, and behaviors are formed from these stored experiences, the subconscious mind is a pivotal force in shaping who we are.

## Subconscious Mind as a Memory Bank

The subconscious mind is like a massive database, constantly recording and storing every experience and memory. To grasp the magnitude of its power, consider this: by the time a person reaches 21 years old, they have stored over 32 million pages of content in their subconscious mind. This far exceeds the page count of the *Encyclopedia Britannica*, which has 32,640 pages. The subconscious mind's capacity to store information is essentially limitless, permanently recording every event, emotion, or perception you've encountered. This enormous volume of information continuously shapes your beliefs, thoughts, and behaviors.

## Why Is the Subconscious Mind More Powerful?

To understand why the subconscious mind is more powerful than both the conscious and unconscious minds, we must look at its key functions:

1. **Link Between the Conscious and Unconscious Minds**: The subconscious mind serves as a bridge, connecting our everyday conscious experiences with the deeper, stored memories of the unconscious mind. It constantly processes the information from our unconscious and reflects it back to us in the form of habits, automatic behaviors, and belief patterns. While we may not be consciously aware of it, the subconscious is continuously influencing our decision-making, actions, and reactions.

2. **Formation of Beliefs and Habits**: The subconscious mind plays a crucial role in the formation of our beliefs and habits. For instance, if you grew up in an environment where success was rewarded and failure

was punished, these experiences are stored in your subconscious. Over time, they become the foundation of your belief system—how you perceive success and failure and how you react to challenges.

3. **Operates Automatically**: While the conscious mind deals with present-moment awareness, the subconscious mind is always at work behind the scenes, controlling involuntary behaviors and emotions. For example, breathing, walking, and driving (after becoming skilled) all fall under the subconscious mind's domain. These automatic processes allow you to focus on conscious tasks while your subconscious handles the routine activities.

4. **Influences Behavior Without Awareness**: One of the key reasons the subconscious mind is so powerful is because it influences your behavior without you being aware of it. You may believe you are acting on conscious choices, but often, your subconscious beliefs and habits are directing your actions. For example, you may consciously desire success, but if your subconscious is programmed with beliefs of inadequacy or fear of failure, you might self-sabotage without even realizing it.

5. **Emotional and Physical Well-being**: The subconscious mind doesn't just store cognitive memories—it also stores emotional memories, which

influence your mental and physical well-being. Traumas, fears, or even positive experiences stored in the subconscious can manifest in your conscious life as anxiety, confidence, or happiness. Many health issues, including chronic pain or stress, can be traced back to deeply rooted subconscious beliefs and emotional imprints.

The subconscious mind is indeed more powerful than the conscious or unconscious minds because it acts as the intermediary between the two, constantly processing, storing, and retrieving vast amounts of information. It forms the core of our belief systems, driving our actions and decisions without our conscious awareness. By understanding and harnessing the power of the subconscious, we can begin to reshape our beliefs, break negative habits, and create lasting change in our lives.

In essence, to change your life, you must work on your subconscious mind—because it is the root of your beliefs, habits, and behaviors.

## The Functions of the Subconscious Mind

The subconscious mind plays a vital role in shaping our beliefs, actions, and overall life outcomes. There are four basic functions of the subconscious mind:

## 1. It Is the Storehouse of Beliefs

The primary function of the subconscious mind is to store and retrieve data, which includes all our memories and past experiences. These stored experiences form the foundation of our beliefs, habits, and behaviors. Since the subconscious mind is the repository for these deeply ingrained beliefs, it can easily overpower our conscious mind and compel us to act according to those beliefs. This is why we often find it difficult to change certain long-held beliefs or behaviors—they are deeply rooted in the subconscious.

For instance, if someone has grown up in an environment where they were consistently told they weren't good enough, that belief is stored in their subconscious mind. As a result, even when they consciously strive for success, their subconscious belief may still drive self-sabotaging behavior.

## 2. It Has Limitless Capacity & Processing Power

The subconscious mind has an almost limitless capacity to store information. It is like a vast memory bank that permanently records everything that ever happens to us. The subconscious mind's strength lies in its ability to simultaneously collect, store, and process vast amounts of data without overwhelming us.

While the conscious mind can focus on only a few things at a time, the subconscious mind processes multiple streams of information simultaneously. This capability enables it to control many aspects of our lives—our beliefs, emotions, mood, and perception—without our awareness. This multitasking ability allows the subconscious mind to quietly govern much of what we do and think, subtly shaping our life experiences and outcomes.

## 3. It Controls Emotions

The subconscious mind is the source of our emotions. Emotions are powerful mental states that arise spontaneously without conscious effort. Since emotions play a key role in influencing our behavior, the subconscious mind can easily direct us by evoking emotional responses that motivate us to take specific actions.

For example, if you subconsciously associate public speaking with fear and anxiety due to a past negative experience, your subconscious mind will trigger those emotions whenever you face a similar situation. These emotions can be so overwhelming that they dictate your behavior, making it difficult to overcome the fear even if you consciously desire to do so.

## 4. It Is Where Mental Programs Are Created and Carried Out

The subconscious mind ensures that we respond consistently with our deeply held beliefs and past experiences by creating and executing mental programs. These mental programs are essentially habitual patterns of thinking, feeling, and acting.

Once established, the subconscious mind continually runs these programs, often without any input from the conscious mind.

For instance, if you have a deeply ingrained belief that you are bad at math, your subconscious mind will create a mental program that reinforces that belief. Consequently, whenever you encounter a math-related task, your subconscious mind will automatically trigger negative thoughts and emotions, leading you to avoid or perform poorly in the task.

The subconscious mind can be seen as a "master program" that governs much of what we say, do, and feel to fit the pattern of our self-concept—a collection of our beliefs about ourselves. However, the same subconscious mind that enforces these programs can also be reprogrammed. If you want to change your deeply rooted mental patterns, you need to work on the subconscious mind to install new programs.

The subconscious mind is a powerful force that shapes our beliefs, emotions, behaviors, and ultimately, our lives. Understanding its functions allows us to recognize how deeply it influences us and how essential it is to engage in reprogramming if we wish to change our life's trajectory. By accessing and reshaping the mental programs stored in the subconscious mind, we can align our beliefs with the outcomes we desire and experience greater control over our lives.

# Chapter 12

# HOW DO OUR BELIEFS DRIVE US?

Our beliefs play a powerful role in shaping our lives. They are deeply ingrained in our subconscious mind and have a significant influence on how we respond to the external environment. The human mind, as we've discussed, is made up of the conscious mind and the subconscious mind, with the latter being responsible for 95% of our responses and actions. This means that the subconscious mind, which is the seat of our beliefs, drives most of our behaviors, decisions, and actions, while the conscious mind, where logic and reasoning reside, plays a relatively small role.

## Beliefs and the Subconscious Mind

Our subconscious mind acts like a fertile soil where the seeds of our beliefs, sown throughout our lives, are planted and grown. These seeds may be positive or negative and are shaped by our experiences, upbringing, and influences from the world around us. Once a belief is established, it begins to generate emotions, and these emotions drive us to act in certain ways.

The subconscious mind does not question the beliefs we plant in it; it simply obeys the commands and instructions given by the conscious mind. For instance, if the conscious mind repeatedly tells itself, "I am not good enough," the subconscious mind will accept this as fact and create behavior patterns that reinforce this belief. As such, the subconscious mind is responsible for creating and running the mental programs that control our actions, often without us being aware of it.

## How Our Beliefs Shape Our Lives

Consider this example: Imagine a child named Tommy who, at a young age, hears from a teacher or parent that he is "not good at mathematics." This comment, though seemingly small, can form the foundation of a belief within Tommy's subconscious mind that he is indeed bad at math. Over time, this belief is reinforced by experiences that support it—failing a quiz, struggling with homework, or hearing others say that math is difficult. Even if Tommy later performs well in a math test, his subconscious mind dismisses it as an exception rather than evidence to the contrary.

As Tommy grows older, this belief manifests in his behavior. He may avoid tasks that involve math, make jokes about his math skills, or even give up before trying. This cycle continues, and Tommy's belief that he is "bad at math" becomes a deeply ingrained mental program that shapes his actions and limits his potential. His belief system has become the driving force behind his inability to succeed in this area of his life.

## The Power of Emotion in Reinforcing Beliefs

Emotions play a critical role in reinforcing beliefs. When Tommy experiences emotions like frustration, shame, or inadequacy related to math, these emotions further solidify his belief that he is bad at it. The more emotionally charged the belief, the more deeply it is ingrained in the subconscious mind. This emotional attachment makes it even harder to change the belief because it becomes part of Tommy's identity.

As an adult, Tommy may find ways to cope with his belief, such as delegating math-related tasks to others or avoiding them altogether. However, until he addresses the root cause—the belief that he is bad at math—he will continue to be driven by this subconscious program. This is true for any belief we hold about ourselves, whether it is related to our abilities, our worth, or our potential for success.

## Breaking the Cycle

The good news is that while our beliefs drive us, we are not powerless to change them. If Tommy recognizes that his belief about math is limiting his potential, he can begin to challenge it. By consciously choosing to replace the negative belief with a positive one—such as "I am capable of learning math"—and reinforcing this new belief through positive experiences and emotions, Tommy can reprogram his subconscious mind.

Changing beliefs requires conscious effort and repetition. Just as beliefs are formed through repeated experiences and reinforcement, they can be changed through the same process. By consciously choosing new thoughts, emotions, and actions, we can create new mental programs that align with our desired outcomes.

## Taking Responsibility for Our Beliefs

It's easy to blame others—parents, teachers, or society—for the beliefs we hold, but ultimately, the responsibility for our lives lies with us. While we may not have been in control of the beliefs that were formed in childhood, as adults, we have the power to change them. We can choose to stop making excuses and take control of our belief system, reprogramming it to reflect the life we want to create.

In conclusion, our beliefs drive us because they are embedded in our subconscious mind, influencing our thoughts, emotions, actions, and ultimately, our results. By recognizing the power of our beliefs and taking responsibility for them, we can break free from limiting patterns and create new, empowering beliefs that lead to positive outcomes.

# Chapter 13

# YOU ARE A VICTIM OF YOUR BELIEFS

Now that we have a comprehensive understanding of what a belief system is, how it works, and how it determines the course of our lives, we can correctly answer the question raised during our case study on the lion. The lion, with its belief system and understanding of its inherent abilities, develops an attitude that makes it a fearless creature. The lion's confidence in its belief system informs how it carries itself, acts, and generally behaves. This is why, when it sees any other animal, the lion is not afraid. It's all about belief.

To develop this kind of attitude in life, we must adopt a positive belief system. This cannot be based on our existing negative beliefs. It must be grounded in something deeper—namely, our "self-identity" (who we are) and our "self-concept" (the mental picture we hold of ourselves). These are the pillars that can reshape our belief system and, consequently, our lives.

## The Power of Belief in Shaping Your Life

Whether you like it or not, you are a victim of your beliefs. The outcome of your life today—whether you are successful, content, or frustrated—has been determined by your belief system. If you want to see different results in your life, you must first change the underlying beliefs that shape your thoughts, actions, and decisions.

Consider this: If you are unhappy, unsatisfied, or feel lost in life, the root cause is often buried deep within your belief system. It is your belief system that is creating the limitations you are experiencing. I speak from experience. Growing up in a poor family of twelve children with uneducated parents, my belief system was deeply entrenched in a poverty mindset. That shaped the way I saw myself and my future.

But when I encountered new beliefs and started to reprogram my mind, my life began to change. I realized that I am a product of the information and faith that I had been exposed to. Once I began feeding my mind with new information and aligning my beliefs with positive outcomes, everything started to shift for me.

## Reprogramming Your Belief System

To see real change in your life, you must go through a process of reprogramming your beliefs. This often means deleting some of the limiting beliefs you currently hold and replacing them with new, empowering ones.

Science has shown that when we change our beliefs, we send different messages to our cells, reprogramming them to express themselves differently. This means that you can transform a pessimistic outlook into an optimistic one by adopting positive mental assertions, ultimately producing lasting positive results in your life.

For instance, consider the classic example of the glass that is filled halfway with water. A pessimist sees it as half-empty, while an optimist sees it as half-full. The glass remains the same, but the perspective changes the experience. Similarly, if you want to change your circumstances, you must change your perception of reality by altering your belief system.

## How to Change Your Belief System

You might wonder, "How do I change my belief system?" The answer lies in picking up a new manual from your Creator—the Bible—and downloading new realities into your mind. By filling your mind with the Word of God, you will start to see yourself in a new light and gain a better understanding of your true identity and purpose.

Your country, culture, and upbringing have significantly shaped your belief system. However, if these factors have contributed to the limitations you are experiencing, it's time to move beyond them. For example, some people define themselves by their nationality, saying things like, "I am Ghanaian, and there's nothing I can do about my circumstances," or "There's no opportunity here in my country." Until you stop limiting yourself by your nationality or culture, you may never unlock your full potential.

While it is true that you are a product of your environment and experiences, you are not defined by them. The limitations you face in life often stem from seeing yourself as being tied to a particular origin, tribe, or custom. If you can shift your mentality and expand your self-concept, you can break free from these limitations and step into your true identity.

## Knowing Your "Self-Identity" and "Self-Concept"

In order to change your belief system, you must first know your "self-identity" and be aware of your "self-concept." These two elements form the foundation of your belief system and, ultimately, your reality. As you continue reading, we will explore these concepts in depth and provide practical steps for reshaping your beliefs to create the life you were destined for.

Transformation begins with understanding who you are and adopting the beliefs that align with your true potential.

# *Chapter 14*

# SELF-CONCEPT

It's not enough to merely know your self-identity; you must also have a clear and empowering mental picture of yourself. This means seeing yourself as God sees you and owning that image. This chapter focuses on understanding and shaping that mental picture, known as your self-concept.

## What Mental Picture Do You Have of "Who You Are" as a Person?

This question delves into your perception of yourself. Do you have a mental image of who you truly are? Self-concept refers to how you think about, evaluate, or perceive yourself. It involves an awareness of oneself and can be understood as your overall mental image of yourself.

According to "yourdictionary.com," self-concept is:

- The way in which you think about yourself and the way in which you see yourself as a person.

- The mental image or perception that one has of oneself.

Lexico defines self-concept as:

- An idea of the self constructed from the beliefs one holds about oneself and the responses of others.

## Components of Self-Concept

Your self-concept is:

- A collection of beliefs about yourself.

- Composed of self-schemas, including your past, present, and future selves.

**Self-schemas** are mental images or frameworks produced in response to stimuli that form the basis for analyzing or responding to other related stimuli. For example, your self-schema helps you process and respond to events you experience.

In general, self-concept answers the question, "Who am I?"— a question rooted in self-identity. However, **self-identity** is not the same as **self-concept**. Self-identity relates to who you are, while self-concept relates to the mental picture you have of yourself.

## Related Terms and Their Distinctions

Several terms are connected to self-concept but have distinct meanings:

- **Self-Perspective:** This refers to how you look at yourself, your mental outlook, or view of yourself.

While it can be used interchangeably with self-concept, self-concept is a more in-depth concept.

- **Self-Awareness:** This is your knowledge of yourself and your worth as a person. It involves recognizing yourself as an individual with unique attributes. Self-awareness should not be confused with consciousness, which is the awareness of your environment and body. Self-awareness, on the other hand, is the recognition of your awareness.

- **Self-Esteem:** This is your belief and pride in yourself—your respect for or favorable opinion of yourself. While self-concept is cognitive (descriptive of oneself, such as "I am intelligent"), self-esteem is evaluative (an opinion about oneself, such as "I feel good because I am intelligent").

- **Self-Perception:** This is the idea you have about the kind of person you are—your awareness of the characteristics that make up your self-concept.

## Building and Creating Your Self-Concept

Your self-concept is essentially your personal perception of your behavior, abilities, and unique characteristics—what you mentally picture when you think of yourself. Where does this mental picture come from? It is built from and shaped by the perception you have of your past, present, and future selves. This is why understanding your self-identity is crucial; it helps you create an accurate and empowering mental picture of who you are.

Your self-concept influences how you think, feel, and behave, impacting your overall sense of well-being. As such, it is vital to shape your self-concept based on your true identity—what God says about you—rather than the negative influences of your past or the opinions of others.

## The 3 Components of Self-Concept

Humanist psychologist Carl Rogers proposed that self-concept comprises three components:

1. The view you have of yourself **(self-image)**

2. How much value you place on yourself **(self-esteem or self-worth)**

3. What you wish you were really like **(ideal self)**

While I agree with Rogers' first two components, I believe the third component—what he terms the "ideal self"—should instead focus on the **real self**. A wish, by definition, is a desire, and desires differ from person to person. Basing self-concept on wishes or desires can create an idealized version of oneself that may not be grounded in reality. Instead, it is more meaningful to focus on the **real self**—the true, authentic version of who you are, based on facts and not just aspirations.

This alternative perspective provides a clearer understanding of self-concept. The components, therefore, should be:

1.  **Self-Image**: The view you have of yourself.

2.  **Self-Esteem/Self-Worth**: How much value you place on yourself.

3.  **Real-Self**: Who you truly are, beyond aspirations or desires.

This makes perfect sense: there is the view you have of yourself (self-image). Then, there's the value you place on that view—whether or not you believe in it (self-esteem or self-worth). Finally, you should have a clear understanding of who you truly are, beyond the view you hold and the value you assign to it, rather than relying on what you wish you could be (ideal-self). As a Scottish proverb wisely says, "If wishes were horses, beggars would ride." This suggests that if merely wishing could make things happen, even the most destitute would have everything they desired. Unfortunately, wishes alone can't bring about change. A wish is merely a desire or hope; therefore, your self-concept shouldn't be built on wishes or hope, but on reality. Let's explore these three components in detail:

# 1. Self-Image

Self-image is fundamentally the idea you have of yourself, encompassing how you see your identity, abilities, qualities, and worth. It is your mental picture of who you are and the way you perceive your personal value. However, as we explore the concept further, we find that self-image can be both accurate and inaccurate, inflated or deflated, and it often doesn't align with objective reality.

## The Nature of Self-Image

According to the dictionary:

- Self-image is the conception you have of yourself, including an assessment of your qualities and personal worth.

- It is how you think about and view yourself, including your identity, abilities, and worth.

The word "conception" here translates to the *idea* you hold about yourself. So, your self-image consists of the thoughts, beliefs, and assumptions you have about who you are. This self-image shapes your view of your own strengths, weaknesses, and worth, influencing how you act and react to the world around you.

## Examples of Self-Image

Consider these examples:

- A woman may see herself as beautiful and intelligent, whether or not that is an accurate perception. To her, this belief shapes her interactions with others and her confidence in social settings. Her self-image becomes a critical factor in how she navigates the world.

- Conversely, someone suffering from anorexia may view themselves as overweight, despite being underweight. In this case, their self-image is distorted and doesn't match reality, but it still governs their behavior, emotions, and decisions.

These examples illustrate that self-image doesn't always align with objective facts. Self-image is based on personal perceptions, which are influenced by internal beliefs, past experiences, and external feedback.

## The Components of Self-Image

Your self-image is a blend of different attributes, including:

- **Physical Characteristics**: How you perceive your body, including your appearance and physical abilities.

- **Personality Traits**: Your view of your character, strengths, weaknesses, and tendencies.

- **Social Roles**: How you see your position in relationships, work, and society.

Each of these factors contributes to how you perceive yourself. However, this perception can be shaped by numerous influences, some of which can distort your self-image either positively or negatively.

## Influences on Self-Image

A person's self-image can be shaped and influenced by various factors, such as:

- **Culture**: Cultural norms and societal standards often dictate what is valued, influencing how we see ourselves.

- **Parental Influences**: The way we were treated and spoken to as children often sets the foundation for how we perceive ourselves later in life.

- **Age and Gender**: Our self-image can evolve with age, and gender norms and expectations can influence how we see ourselves.

- **Appearance**: How we view our physical selves, including body image, can heavily influence our overall self-image.

- **Friends and Social Circles**: The opinions and treatment we receive from others play a role in how we view ourselves.

- **Media**: Media representations of beauty, success, and value can warp our self-image if we internalize unrealistic standards.

- **Relationships**: Positive or negative relationships can shape how we see ourselves in relation to others.

- **Abuse and Trauma**: Negative experiences, especially from abuse, can deeply distort self-image, leading to feelings of worthlessness or self-blame.

- **Income and Social Status**: Our socioeconomic standing can impact our sense of worth and achievement, shaping how we see ourselves in the world.

## The Impact of Self-Image

The way you see yourself affects how you interact with the world. A positive self-image can lead to confidence, healthy relationships, and a proactive approach to life. A negative self-image, however, can result in low self-esteem, anxiety, depression, and self-sabotaging behaviors.

Your self-image is the lens through which you view your potential and possibilities. If you have an accurate and balanced self-image, you are more likely to live authentically, accept yourself, and pursue your goals with clarity. However, if your self-image is distorted, you may struggle with self-doubt, fear of failure, or an inability to recognize your true worth.

Your self-image is the idea or set of beliefs you hold about yourself, including your qualities, abilities, and worth. It may be influenced by factors such as upbringing, culture, appearance, relationships, and media, but it doesn't necessarily reflect reality. Understanding and cultivating a healthy self-image is crucial for personal growth, confidence, and a positive outlook on life. Recognizing the impact of external influences on self-image allows you to critically evaluate and reshape how you see yourself, leading to a more authentic and empowered version of you.

## 2. Self-Esteem or Self-Worth

Self-esteem, also known as self-worth, reflects how much value you place on yourself. It influences your self-perception, confidence, and belief in your own abilities. Self-esteem is not static and can be shaped by various internal and external factors throughout your life.

### Definition of Self-Esteem

The dictionary defines self-esteem as:

- Confidence in one's own worth or abilities; self-respect.

- A realistic respect for or favorable impression of oneself.

This means that self-esteem is the belief and trust you have in your own importance and abilities. It determines whether you feel confident and capable or whether you feel inadequate and unworthy.

## High Self-Esteem vs. Low Self-Esteem

- **High Self-Esteem:** If you have high self-esteem, you hold a positive view of yourself. You are confident in your abilities, have a strong sense of self-worth, and are generally optimistic about life. This leads to a mindset where challenges are seen as opportunities, and you are less affected by external validation or criticism.

- **Low Self-Esteem:** If you have low self-esteem, you doubt your abilities and often compare yourself unfavorably to others. This negative view of yourself can lead to feelings of inadequacy, unhappiness, and pessimism. Individuals with low self-esteem tend to expect the worst from situations, avoid risks, and may develop self-destructive habits.

## Factors Influencing Self-Esteem

Self-esteem doesn't develop in a vacuum; it is influenced by several factors that can either build or erode your confidence and self-worth.

## 1. Comparison with Others

One of the most common influences on self-esteem is comparison. If you frequently compare yourself to others and find yourself lacking (e.g., less successful, less attractive, poorer), it can lead to negative self-esteem. On the contrary, if you compare yourself favorably to others (e.g., more successful, happier, richer), it can boost your self-esteem. However, it's important to note that constant comparison can be detrimental, as it often leads to feelings of inadequacy.

## 2. Response and Reaction from Others

The way others react to you can have a profound impact on your self-esteem. Positive reinforcement, such as praise, admiration, and validation, boosts self-esteem, while negative reactions like criticism, rejection, and neglect can undermine it. The feedback we receive from others, especially those we respect or care about, shapes how we perceive our worth.

## 3. Identification with Others

The extent to which you identify with certain groups or individuals can influence your self-esteem. If you associate yourself with a group that is privileged or holds a high status in society, your self-esteem may rise. Conversely, identifying with a less privileged or stigmatized group may result in lower self-esteem. Your sense of belonging and your role in society play a significant role in shaping how you feel about yourself.

## 4. Social Roles

Your self-esteem is also affected by the social roles you occupy. Holding a prestigious or respected role in society (e.g., doctor, lawyer, engineer) tends to boost self-esteem. On the other hand, holding a stigmatized or less prestigious role (e.g., prisoner, unemployed person) can lower self-esteem. The positions you hold and the way society view those roles contribute to how you perceive your own worth.

## 5. Parental Influence

The relationship you had with your parents or primary caregivers plays a critical role in shaping your self-esteem. Positive reinforcement, love, and encouragement during childhood create a foundation for healthy self-esteem. In contrast, a negative, neglectful, or abusive environment can damage self-esteem and create a negative self-image. Parental influence often sets the stage for how individuals relate to themselves and others in adulthood.

## Evaluation and Self-Esteem

Self-esteem involves a degree of evaluation. You assess your qualities, compare yourself to others, and gauge how much you value yourself. This evaluation can lead to either a positive or negative view of yourself. For example:

- **Positive Evaluation:** Leads to high self-esteem, where you recognize your strengths, accept your flaws, and remain confident in your abilities.

- **Negative Evaluation:** Leads to low self-esteem, where you focus on your weaknesses, doubt your abilities, and feel unworthy of success or happiness.

## Impact of Self-Esteem

Your level of self-esteem affects almost every aspect of your life, including:

- **Relationships:** Individuals with high self-esteem tend to have healthier relationships because they value themselves and set healthy boundaries. Those with low self-esteem may struggle with relationships, as they may allow others to mistreat them or constantly seek validation.

- **Career Success:** High self-esteem drives individuals to take risks, pursue opportunities, and face challenges with confidence, leading to higher success rates. Low self-esteem can hinder career growth due to fear of failure and reluctance to seize opportunities.

- **Mental Health:** People with low self-esteem are more susceptible to depression, anxiety, and other mental health issues. High self-esteem promotes resilience and emotional well-being.

Self-esteem, or self-worth, is a vital component of your self-concept. It is the belief you have in your own value and abilities, which influences your confidence, relationships, and overall outlook on life. By understanding the factors that shape your self-esteem, you can work towards building a healthier, more positive view of yourself. Emphasizing self-worth leads to a more fulfilling life, while negative self-esteem can hold you back from reaching your full potential.

## 3. Real-Self

The *real-self* is about understanding and embracing who you truly are, as opposed to your *ideal-self*, which is based on desires, hopes, or what you wish to be. The *real-self* is grounded in facts and reflects your true nature, talents, limitations, and strengths, while the *ideal-self* is often a projection of what you aspire to be but may not be grounded in reality.

**Difference Between Real-Self and Ideal-Self**

- **Real-Self** is based on the reality of who you are, what you've accomplished, and the person you are at this moment. It encompasses your current strengths, weaknesses, emotions, and personal qualities that make you who you are.

- **Ideal-Self** is a vision of the person you want to become. It reflects your aspirations, desires, and goals, which may or may not be achievable depending on your circumstances, beliefs, and efforts.

While the *real-self* is based on factual self-awareness, the *ideal-self* can sometimes be unrealistic, influenced by external pressures, societal expectations, or personal fantasies. When there is a significant gap between your self-image (how you currently perceive yourself) and your *ideal-self* (what you wish to be), it can cause dissatisfaction and negatively impact your self-esteem.

**Why Knowing Your Real-Self Is Important**

Understanding and accepting your *real-self* is essential because it allows you to:

1. **Build a Strong Self-Concept:** When you embrace your *real-self*, you develop a more grounded and accurate perception of who you are. This, in turn, strengthens your self-concept, allowing you to navigate life with greater clarity and self-confidence.

2. **Set Realistic Goals:** Knowing your *real-self* helps you set goals that align with your true abilities and interests. This enables you to pursue objectives that are meaningful and achievable, leading to greater fulfillment and success.

3. **Enhance Self-Esteem:** When there is congruence between your self-image and your *real-self*, your self-esteem improves because you are no longer striving to live up to an unrealistic standard. Accepting who you are helps you value yourself more genuinely.

4. **Improve Mental Well-being:** Embracing your *real-self* promotes mental and emotional well-being, as you are less likely to experience the frustration and anxiety

that comes from constantly comparing yourself to an unattainable ideal.

## Self-Concept and Real-Self Connection

Your *real-self* forms the foundation of your self-concept. It shapes the way you perceive yourself and influences your self-worth. By aligning your self-concept with your *real-self*, you foster a healthier relationship with yourself and can grow into the best version of who you truly are.

In the next chapter, we will dive deeper into understanding your *real-self* under the topic of *self-identity*, which will provide a more comprehensive exploration of how to discover and embrace who you genuinely are. This will equip you to lead a more authentic and purpose-driven life.

## High-Level Summary

## 1. Self-Image: The View You Have of Yourself

Self-image refers to how you perceive yourself. It is the mental picture you have of yourself in terms of physical appearance, personality traits, abilities, and roles. Self-image can be influenced by a variety of factors such as personal experiences, societal expectations, and feedback from others.

Your self-image is not always accurate or aligned with reality. You may view yourself in a negative or distorted way due to past failures, criticism, or societal pressures. Alternatively, you might have an inflated self-image based on false perceptions of your abilities or worth. Developing a healthy, balanced self-image is crucial to personal growth and well-being.

## 2. Self-Esteem: The Value You Place on Yourself

Self-esteem is the emotional and evaluative aspect of self-concept. It is the value or worth you place on the self-image you have created. Self-esteem is how you feel about yourself based on the perception of who you are.

High self-esteem means you value yourself positively, have confidence in your abilities, and believe in your worth. Low self-esteem, on the other hand, can lead to feelings of inadequacy, insecurity, and self-doubt. Building self-esteem requires recognizing your strengths, embracing your weaknesses, and affirming your value as a person, regardless of external validation.

## 3. Real-Self: Who You Really Are

The real-self is your true, authentic self, independent of any idealized version or wishful thinking. It is based on facts and reflects your actual abilities, character, and identity.

While the "ideal self" focuses on what you wish to be, the "real self" focuses on understanding and accepting who you truly are at your core. This involves an honest appraisal of your strengths, weaknesses, desires, and limitations. Knowing your real-self provides a stable foundation upon which you can build your life, free from unrealistic expectations or external pressures.

## Why Focus on the Real-Self Instead of the Ideal-Self?

The concept of the "ideal self" is built on desires, which can be fleeting and based on external factors. Pursuing an idealized version of yourself can lead to dissatisfaction and frustration, as it often involves striving for unattainable goals or living up to societal standards that may not reflect your true nature. The Scottish proverb, *"If wishes were horses, beggars would ride,"* emphasizes the futility of basing life on mere wishes.

Focusing on your real-self, on the other hand, grounds you in reality. It allows you to accept yourself for who you are, embrace your strengths, and work on your weaknesses. By building your self-concept on the real self, you cultivate resilience, self-acceptance, and a sense of purpose that is rooted in authenticity, not fantasy.

A healthy self-concept integrates an accurate self-image, a balanced sense of self-worth, and a deep understanding of the real-self. It is based on truth, not on wishful thinking. By recognizing who you truly are and valuing that person, you set yourself on a path of personal growth, fulfillment, and lasting success.

In conclusion, self-concept is the composite of your self-schemas, which interact with three critical components: your *self-image* (how you perceive yourself), your *self-esteem* (the value you place on yourself), and your *real-self* (who you truly are). Together, these components form the complete picture of your identity, shaping the "whole" self. It is important to distinguish the *real-self* from the *ideal-self*, as the *real-self* is grounded in factual self-awareness, while the *ideal-self* is based on desires and wishes that may not reflect reality.

Self-concept also encompasses your past, present, and future selves:

- **Your past-self** represents your history, but it should not dictate your present.

- **Your present-self** is your current state—*the now*—and it is the only moment you can actively shape and influence.

- **Your future-self** refers to your possible-selves—what you might become, aspire to be, or fear becoming.

While it is natural to have aspirations and concerns about the future, your *real-self*—who you genuinely are—should be the primary catalyst for your behavior and the driving force behind your life's ultimate outcomes. Embrace your *real-self* to cultivate a healthy, balanced self-concept that will lead you to live an authentic, purpose-driven life.

# *Chapter 15*

# SELF-IDENTITY

## Who Are You?

This question addresses the core of identity and is the foundation upon which your life is built. Until you can answer it, living a life of peak performance and maximum productivity will be difficult. Self-identity consists of two key parts:

1. **Understanding Your Identity:**

   Who are you? Do you truly know your identity, or are you merely assuming one? This is not a question of what you do, but of who you are. Discovering your true self will enable you to fully become it.

2. **Understanding Your Origin & Source:**

   Where do you come from? Do you truly know your origin and source? This is not about ethnicity or nationality—it's about your creation. By understanding where you came from, you can uncover your abilities, strengths, and potential.

Many people on earth don't truly know who they are. This is not about your job or title—it's not about saying, "I am an engineer" or "I am an administrator." Most people lack a clear sense of self and, as a result, live their lives as someone they are not. Studies have shown that about 99% of the world's population suffer from an identity crisis. The tall wants to be short, the short wants to be tall. The slim wants to be fat, and the fat wants to be slim. The old wishes to be young, while the young longs to be older. It's a never-ending cycle of identity confusion.

Some people are still caught up in the theory of evolution. Charles Darwin's theory, first proposed in 1859, suggests that organisms evolve over time due to changes in heritable physical or behavioral traits. According to this theory, mankind evolved from apes. Sadly, this theory continues to be taught in schools.

Who you think you are profoundly affects how you live your life. I often ask those who believe in evolution: "If man evolved from apes, why have we not evolved into something else?" To this day, no one has provided a satisfactory answer.

There's a well-known story about a chicken farmer who found an eagle's egg. He placed the egg alongside his chickens' eggs, and eventually, the eagle hatched. Growing up with the chicks, the young eagle imitated them, believing itself to be a chicken. Since the chicks could only fly short distances, the eagle learned to do the same. Its belief system limited its potential, and it lived like a chicken, never realizing its true nature as an eagle.

One day, the eagle saw a bird soaring high in the sky and asked the chickens, "Who is that?" The chickens responded, "That's the eagle, the king of birds. It belongs to the sky, but we belong to the earth; we're just chickens." And so, the eagle spent the rest of its life thinking it was a chicken, living and dying as such.

It's a sad story, but it reflects the lives of many people who live like chickens when they were created to be eagles. Until you know who you are and where you come from, you will live as someone you are not. Like the eagle in the story, if you do not know your identity, you will think, talk, and act like something you were never meant to be.

Many people today believe they are merely advanced forms of apes, and so they live and act according to what they believe. But here's the truth: a lion that believes it's a dog will live like a dog. Who do you believe you are? Your beliefs about your identity, origin, and source will shape your understanding of yourself and what you are capable of.

You've heard it said many times: "Knowledge is power." This is true, but it's not just what you know—it's also what you do with that knowledge. The reason you are where you are in life is tied to what you do or don't know, and what you do or don't apply. So, the big question remains: Who are you?

Friends, I won't deceive you. I believe in a supernatural God who created man in His own image and likeness to reign and have dominion on earth as kings. I believe that man was born to reign in life. I believe that man is not an ordinary being but is destined for greatness.

We mentioned in Chapter 1 that lions share similar characteristics and abilities that distinguish them from other animals, causing them to think and act alike. Similarly, human beings also possess distinctive traits, features, and inherent abilities that define who we are. Understanding and recognizing these qualities will shape how we think about ourselves, how we see ourselves, and ultimately, who we truly are.

With this in mind, human beings possess four distinct traits, features, and abilities that set us apart from all other living things created by God. As human beings, we are:

## 1. Created in the Image and Likeness of God

The Bible, in Genesis 1, says:

*Then God said, "Let us make mankind in our image, in our likeness, so that they may rule over the fish in the sea and the birds in the sky, over the livestock and all the wild animals, and over all the creatures that move along the ground." So God created mankind in His own image, in the image of God He created them; male and female He created them.* —Genesis 1:26-27 (NIV)

You were created in the very image and likeness of God. You are not a biological accident. It doesn't matter if you were born under difficult or questionable circumstances—God had a plan for your conception. He created you in His image and likeness, making you a child of God.

The term "image" means a "physical likeness or representation of a person, animal, or thing." It means a copy, an exact replica. Therefore, you are an exact copy of God.

What does this mean? It means you are a "mini-god." This is not blasphemy or heresy—it is the truth. The Bible says: *"I have said, Ye are gods; and all of you are children of the most High."* —Psalm 82:6 (KJV)

According to the Brown-Driver-Briggs Hebrew and English Lexicon, the Hebrew word translated as "gods" here is *eloheem*, the same word used for "God" in Genesis 1:1: *"In the beginning God created the heaven and the earth."* —Genesis 1:1 (KJV)

So, it is no mistake; it is a fact. You are a "god" because you were created in the image and likeness of God, the One who made you. Therefore, you carry the DNA and nature of God, the Creator of the entire universe.

The Bible further states, *"...and all of you are the children of the most High."* When a lion gives birth, it produces a lion;

when a dog gives birth, it produces a dog. Similarly, when God gives birth, He produces a "god." You are a child of God. However, it is disheartening that, despite this truth, many people still live mediocre lives. Why? The answer is found in Psalm 82:5: *"They know not, neither will they understand; they walk on in darkness: all the foundations of the earth are out of course."* —Psalm 82:5 (KJV)

It is because *"they know not..."* And the consequence of not knowing is revealed in Psalm 82:7: *"But you will die like mere mortals; you will fall like every other ruler."* —Psalm 82:7 (NIV)

Friends, it is time for you to live as a "god" so that you do not die as a mere mortal. The seed of God is within you. You are not an ordinary person.


## 2.  Uniquely and Wonderfully Made by God

According to Psalm 139:

*"I will praise thee; for I am fearfully and wonderfully made: marvellous are thy works; and that my soul knoweth right well."* —Psalm 139:14 (KJV)

You are fearfully and wonderfully made by God. Out of the over 7.9 billion people in the world today, there is no one exactly like you. There never has been, and there never will be. God took His time to create you in a special and unique way. No two human beings share the same tongue, voice, or fingerprints. They may be similar, but they are not identical. This clearly shows that you are uniquely made by God.

Scientists tell us that over 500 million sperm are contained in the semen released during sexual intercourse, and each one competes to fertilize the woman's egg. The fact that you were born means you were the one who came out victorious. You are wonderful, and it's time for you to embrace your uniqueness.

## 3. Given Dominion Over the Whole Earth

The Bible says:

*"And God said, Let us make man in our image, after our likeness: and let them have dominion over the fish of the sea, and over the fowl of the air, and over the cattle, and over all the earth, and over every creeping thing that creepeth upon the earth."* —Genesis 1:26 (KJV)

This verse makes it clear that God has given you dominion over everything on earth. To have dominion means to have "rule or power to rule; sovereign authority or control." When God created man, He placed him on earth to have dominion over it. You are meant to govern and reign as a king on earth—dominating in your area of expertise, whether it be a pursuit, a field of study, or a skill in which you have devoted much time and effort and in which you have become proficient.

What does this mean? It means that man is ultimately responsible for what happens on earth. You are responsible for the outcome of your life and for what happens on the earth. Therefore, man can only permit God to influence his activities on earth through prayer by asking for His guidance.

## 4. The Highest of God's Creation

The Bible, speaking in Psalm 8, says:

*"What is man that You are mindful of him, and the son of man that You visit him? For You have made him a little lower than the angels, and You have crowned him with glory and honor. You have made him to have dominion over the works of Your hands; You have put all things under his feet."* —Psalm 8:4-6 (NKJV)

According to the Brown-Driver-Briggs Hebrew and English Lexicon, the Hebrew word translated as "angels" here is *eloheem*, the same word used for "God" in Genesis 1:1: *"In the beginning God created the heaven and the earth."* —Genesis 1:1 (KJV)

Therefore, Psalm 8:4-6 can be understood as:

*"What is man that You are mindful of him, and the son of man that You visit him? For You have made him a little lower than God, and You have crowned him with glory and honor. You have made him to have dominion over the works of Your*

*hands; You have put all things under his feet."* —Psalm 8:4-6 (NKJV)

No wonder the New Living Translation renders it this way:

*"What are mere mortals that you should think about them, human beings that you should care for them? Yet you made them only a little lower than God and crowned them with glory and honor. You gave them charge of everything you made, putting all things under their authority."* —Psalm 8:4-6 (NLT)

Man is the highest of God's creation—God made him just a little lower than Himself. *"You made them only a little lower than God."* This means that man shares abilities with God and operates in the same class as God. You are crowned with glory and power and given dominion over the works of God's hands. You are entrusted with the authority over everything God created.

As human beings, we possess the unique ability of imagination—the capacity to envision future possibilities by creating mental images or pictures in our minds. Animals do not share this ability. Man can think constructively, combining knowledge and information acquired over time to produce tangible results and inventions. Why? Because man is the pinnacle of God's creation. This is your position and your nature. Believe it and start living from this reality onward. You are blessed.

Jesus, speaking in John 3:31, says:

*"He who comes from above is above all; he who is of the earth is earthly and speaks of the earth. He who comes from heaven is above all."* —John 3:31 (NKJV)

This Scripture further affirms that your origin is not of the earth. You are from above. Your citizenship is not earthly but heavenly. Just as God is not of the earth, neither are you, because you are His child. Though you were born on earth, your true origin is divine. You are here by divine arrangement.

It is crucial that you know your origin or source—where you came from. Your source determines the resources available to you. Until you understand where you come from, you cannot fully know who you are. There is an old proverb from the Akan tribe in Ghana that says, *"To know where you are going, you must know where you come from."* Your destination and future are shaped by understanding your origin.

I am confident that you now know exactly who you are and where you come from. Knowing that God is your source—and God alone—you can live to fulfill your destiny and experience positive outcomes and success in life.

# Chapter 16

# HOW TO REPROGRAM YOUR BELIEFS SYSTEM

One of the most common questions I'm asked when discussing belief systems is: *Can I reprogram my beliefs?* The answer is, absolutely! However, it's important to understand that your core beliefs do not exist or operate in isolation. They interact with and reinforce one another. Therefore, changing one belief will often affect the entire belief system. If that change impacts a core belief, it can potentially disrupt the usual flow or operation of the entire system. Similarly, when a set of beliefs is altered, other parts of the belief system must realign to restore coherence. As a result, beliefs are usually reprogrammed as a set, rather than individually, because they are interconnected.

At this point, it's essential to recall that we previously discussed the three distinct levels of the human mind: the conscious mind, the subconscious mind, and the unconscious mind. These levels work together to create your reality, as perceived through your beliefs, shaping your thoughts, actions, responses, and reactions.

To recap, the subconscious mind is sandwiched between the conscious and unconscious minds. On a basic level, your conscious mind interacts with the world around you and your inner self (your "inner person" or "inner life") through thoughts, speech, images, physical orientation, and more. Meanwhile, your subconscious mind stores your recent memories and maintains continuous contact with the unconscious mind, which holds all of your past memories and experiences. It is from these past memories and experiences that your beliefs, habits, behaviors, and emotions are formed. This process forms the foundation of your belief system, making the subconscious mind incredibly powerful.

Thus, the subconscious mind is the place where reprogramming takes place.


**Your Mindset**

By definition, *mindset* is:

- A fixed mental attitude or disposition that predetermines a person's response to and interpretation of situations.

- The ideas and attitudes with which a person approaches a situation, especially when these are seen as being difficult to alter.

In other words, your mindset is a fixed mental attitude or disposition that shapes how you respond to and interpret situations. Your mindset is the mechanism that executes your belief system. It influences the way you think, shape your opinions, and impact the beliefs you form. This is why changing your mindset can be extremely difficult. However, if I can change your mindset, I will have succeeded in changing your belief system.

Your mindset affects your conscious, subconscious, and unconscious minds. In fact, it plays a critical role in determining the outcomes of your life. To effectively reprogram your belief system, the battlefield is your mindset. Therefore, gaining dominion and control over your life requires that you be intentional and serious about protecting your mindset.

Before you can protect a negative mindset, you must first reprogram it. Reprogramming your mindset involves empowering it with positive beliefs. Once this is accomplished, you will begin producing more positive thoughts, ideas, and emotions, which will in turn lead to positive actions and outcomes. These changes will foster habits that shape your character and propel you towards a fulfilling destiny, helping you to live the life you have always envisioned.

## Anatomy of the Human Mind

The table below provides a complete breakdown of the human mind, distinctively classified into three levels of awareness: the conscious mind, the subconscious mind, and the unconscious mind. Understanding the functions and distinctions between each part of the mind will better prepare you for the effective application of techniques required to reprogram negative and limiting belief systems.

| CONSCIOUS MIND | SUBCONSCIOUS MIND | UNCONSCIOUS MIND |
| --- | --- | --- |
| 1. Very Small % of the Mind (Approx. 5-12%) | 1. Very Large % of the Mind (Approx. 80-90%) | 1. Very Small % of the Mind (Approx. 5-10%) |
| 2. To Understand | 2. To Protect and Be Right (Acts as the "Hard Drive" of your mind) | 2. To Survive |
| 3. Short-Term Memory | 3. Long-Term Memory (Remembered Trauma) | 3. Permanent Memory Storage (Forgotten Trauma) |

| CONSCIOUS MIND | SUBCONSCIOUS MIND | UNCONSCIOUS MIND |
| --- | --- | --- |
| 4. We Spend Most Time Here | 4. Developmental Stages (DNA) | 4. Early Impressions (In Utero, Birth, 1st Year) |
| 5. Rational and Reasoning (Judgment, Logic & Sequential) | 5. Semi-Automatic Physiological Systems (Involuntary Body Functions, Fight-or-Flight Responses) | 5. Automatic Physiological Systems (Controls automatic body functions like breathing, heartbeat, digestion, immune system) |
| 6. Limited Abilities (Requires effort & energy) | 6. Incredibly Powerful (Much more powerful than the conscious mind. Harnessing this power can dramatically change your life) | 6. Incredible Benefits (Body System Regeneration) |

| CONSCIOUS MIND | SUBCONSCIOUS MIND | UNCONSCIOUS MIND |
| --- | --- | --- |
| 7. Intellectual, Thinking, Planning, Analyzing, Decisions | 7. Limitless Creativity, Visualization, Insight (Imaginative, Mental Imagery, Intuition) | 7. Primal Instinct, Instinctual Responses |
| 8. Negative Self-Talk & Self-Esteem | 8. Self-Talk, Self-Healing, Higher Self | 8. Highest Self |
| 9. Often in Past or Future Tense | 9. Often in Present Tense & Always in the "Now" | 9. Access to Collective Consciousness |
| 10. Personality (Temperamental) | 10. Protective (Real or Imagined) | 10. The "Core" of Who You Are |
| 11. Body, Physical Connection | 11. Soul, Spiritual Connection | 11. Spiritual Connection (Drives the Dreaming State) |

| CONSCIOUS MIND | SUBCONSCIOUS MIND | UNCONSCIOUS MIND |
| --- | --- | --- |
| | 12. Creator of Limiting Beliefs (Says you are not good enough) | 12. Creator of General Beliefs (Holds beliefs about the world and self) |
| 13. Mini-Processor | 13. Super-Processor | |
| 14. Limited Space | 14. Unlimited Space | |
| 15. Willpower Resides Here (Easily overridden when emotions are high) | 15. Thoughts, Feelings, and Emotions Come from Here (Easily override conscious will when emotions are high) | |
| 16. Superficial Ideas (Sets Goals - Knows What You Want) | 16. Desires, Goals, Career, Dreams, Success (Knows | |

| CONSCIOUS MIND | SUBCONSCIOUS MIND | UNCONSCIOUS MIND |
| --- | --- | --- |
| | the path to success) | |
| 17. Stress Source | 17. Stress-Free, Inner Peace (Tells you to relax) | |
| 18. Likes/Dislikes | 18. Relationship Patterns (Love, Trust, Insecurity, Rejection, Fears, Failure) | |
| | 19. Accessed via Deep Thought & Meditation (Requires meditation to harness its power) | |
| | 20. All Experiences Are Stored Here | |

| CONSCIOUS MIND | SUBCONSCIOUS MIND | UNCONSCIOUS MIND |
| --- | --- | --- |
|  | 21. Behaviors, Attitudes, Addictions, and Habits Reside Here |  |

## Technique to Reprogram the Subconscious Mind

There are several techniques that can be used to reprogram the subconscious mind. Among others, I have identified the following eight techniques:

1. **Recognize the Problem**

   - Identify negative and limiting beliefs that are hindering your progress. This is the first and most crucial step in the reprogramming process.

2. **Think God's Thoughts**

   - Align your thoughts with positive, empowering beliefs that reflect God's promises and truths. Replace negative thoughts with those that uplift and inspire.

3. **Visualization**

- Use mental imagery to vividly imagine your desired outcomes. Visualization helps create new neural pathways in the brain, reinforcing positive beliefs.

4. **Positive Affirmations**

- Repeat carefully crafted, positive statements that reflect your desired beliefs and outcomes. Affirmations help reprogram the subconscious mind through repetition.

5. **Positive Self-Talk**

- Engage in encouraging and uplifting internal dialogue. Positive self-talk can counteract negative beliefs and reinforce positive ones.

6. **Gratitude and Appreciation**

- Cultivate a habit of expressing gratitude for what you have and what you desire. Gratitude shifts your focus to the positive aspects of life and strengthens positive beliefs.

7. **Create a Vision Board (Dream Board)**

- Design a visual representation of your goals, desires, and dreams. A vision board helps you focus on your aspirations and keeps them at the forefront of your mind.

8. **Meditation**

- Engage in deep, focused thought or contemplation. Meditation allows you to quiet the mind, access the subconscious, and implant positive beliefs.

By *technique*, I mean a practical method, skill, procedure, or approach that can be used to reprogram negative and limiting belief systems. We will discuss each of these eight techniques in detail in the succeeding chapters.

## Succinct Summary

Here's a succinct summary of the key points:

### Understanding the Reprogramming Process

Reprogramming your belief system is not only possible but essential for personal growth and achieving your goals. Your belief system is a complex network of interconnected beliefs that shape your thoughts, actions, and ultimately your life. When you change one belief, it often affects the entire belief system, leading to a realignment of other related beliefs. This is why reprogramming beliefs is usually more effective when done as a set rather than individually.

To successfully reprogram your belief system, it's crucial to understand the structure of the mind, which consists of the conscious mind, subconscious mind, and unconscious mind.

The subconscious mind, where beliefs are stored and reinforced, is the key area for reprogramming efforts.

## Mindset: The Execution Mechanism of Your Belief System

Your mindset, defined as a fixed mental attitude or disposition, plays a critical role in how you perceive and respond to situations. It serves as the mechanism that executes your belief system, influencing your thoughts, opinions, and actions. Therefore, reprogramming your belief system begins with changing your mindset. A positive, empowered mindset will lead to positive beliefs, which in turn will produce positive outcomes in your life.

## Anatomy of the Human Mind

To effectively reprogram your belief system, it's important to understand the different levels of the human mind and their functions:

1. **Conscious Mind:**

   - Comprises about 5-12% of the mind.

   - Handles understanding, rational thinking, planning, and decision-making.

   - Limited abilities, often focused on short-term memory and superficial ideas.

2. **Subconscious Mind:**

   - Comprises about 80-90% of the mind.

- Acts as the "hard drive," storing long-term memories, emotions, and beliefs.

- Incredibly powerful and holds the key to reprogramming beliefs.

- Influences behaviors, attitudes, and habits, and is accessed through deep thought and meditation.

3. **Unconscious Mind:**

- Comprises about 5-10% of the mind.

- Focuses on survival, automatic physiological systems, and primal instincts.

- Stores permanent memories and influences instinctual responses.

Reprogramming your belief system is a powerful way to take control of your life and achieve your goals. By understanding the structure of your mind and employing techniques such as visualization, positive affirmations, and meditation, you can transform your negative and limiting beliefs into positive and empowering ones. This process will lead to a mindset that supports your growth, success, and fulfillment, enabling you to live the life you have always envisioned.

# Chapter 17

# RECOGNIZE THE PROBLEM

Recognizing the impact of negative and limiting beliefs is the most crucial step in reprogramming the subconscious mind. You cannot solve a problem you don't know exists or refuse to acknowledge. What you do not accept, you cannot correct. God issued a serious warning in the Scriptures:

*"My people are destroyed for lack of knowledge."* —Hosea 4:6 (KJV)

Many people today are struggling because they lack knowledge. In this context, what does knowledge mean? According to the Brown-Driver-Briggs Hebrew and English Lexicon, the Hebrew word used for "knowledge" here is *da'ath*, which translates to "knowledge, perception, skill, discernment, understanding, wisdom." It's unfortunate that many are disoriented today without realizing it. If they could only recognize the problem, they would find the solution. Their downfall isn't because something is out to get them, but because they lack knowledge, understanding, and discernment. They fail to perceive the problem and lack the wisdom to recognize it. You've likely heard the saying, *"A problem identified is a problem half-solved."*

If your life isn't going as planned, despite following all the rules, doing the right things, and adhering to principles—if you've dotted all the i's and crossed all the t's—there's a good chance you're running a subconscious program that's determining your life's outcome. It's time to examine your belief system. If you find yourself getting nervous or even sick when it's time to file your taxes, unable to stand up to a bully at home or work, feeling lost, unhappy, and confused, or repeatedly facing the same miserable situations, it's likely that a negative or limiting belief system in your subconscious mind is causing your problems and shaping your life. In short, I'm advising you to check your belief system. Life follows patterns created over the years by what you choose to believe. Your first step toward change is to use your pattern-detecting conscious mind to identify the programs that need to be changed.

Once you've recognized the problem, the next step is to examine the pattern. You may or may not be able to trace its origin or understand how it started, but don't fret if you can't pinpoint the source—what's most important is being aware of it. Once you recognize and identify the problem, you'll be ready to use any of the succeeding seven techniques to address it.

So, how do you recognize the problem? To identify your negative or limiting beliefs, and uncover the beliefs holding you back, ask yourself questions like these:

1. **Which of my core beliefs, ideas, and habits are preventing me from living the life I want?**

   - Consider any beliefs that make you feel stuck, fearful, or limited in your potential.

2. **Which of my core beliefs, ideas, and habits am I now starting to question?**

   - Reflect on the beliefs you've recently begun to doubt or challenge.

3. **Why have I started questioning these beliefs, ideas, and habits?**

   - Explore the reasons behind your doubts. Have new experiences or insights prompted you to rethink your perspective?

4. **What effect or impact have these beliefs, ideas, and habits had on me, my life, and my future?**

   - Assess how these beliefs have shaped your life so far. Have they helped or hindered your progress?

5. **Which beliefs, ideas, and habits have I been exposed to over the years that I want to eradicate from my subconscious mind?**

   - Identify any negative influences from your past that you wish to eliminate.

6. **Which beliefs, ideas, and habits have I encountered recently that I want to deeply ingrain in my subconscious mind?**

   - Focus on the positive beliefs and habits you want to adopt.

7. **Which of my beliefs, ideas, and habits are stopping me from making progress in the direction I desire?**

   - Pinpoint specific beliefs that are blocking your growth.

8. **Which environments or associations have I been exposed to over the years that are not helping me grow in the direction I want to go?**

   - Evaluate the influence of your surroundings and relationships on your personal development.

9. **Which environments or associations can I expose myself to from now on that will help me grow in the direction I want to become?**

   - Seek out positive environments and relationships that support your goals.

10. **What kind of person was I until now?**

   - Reflect on the person you've been, shaped by your past beliefs and experiences.

11. **What kind of person am I right now?**

- Consider who you are today, acknowledging both strengths and areas for growth.

12. **What kind of person do I want to become?**

- Define the person you aspire to be, guided by positive beliefs and values.

## Analyzing Your Responses

Your answers may not immediately identify your negative and limiting beliefs, but keep asking, reviewing, and reflecting on your beliefs until you recognize your existing belief system. However, it's essential to re-view, re-examine, and re-analyze your perspective on things and life in general. Be very honest with yourself during this process of reviewing, examining, and analyzing.

Your answers to these questions will provide insight into the belief systems that govern your life. However, identifying these beliefs is just the beginning. The next step is to critically analyze and reflect on your responses. Be honest with yourself as you examine the patterns that emerge. Understanding these patterns will help you recognize the beliefs that need to be changed.

**Taking Action**

Once you've identified the limiting beliefs, you can begin the process of reprogramming your subconscious mind using techniques such as positive affirmations, visualization, meditation, and gratitude practices. The key is to replace negative beliefs with positive, empowering ones that align with the person you want to become.

By taking the time to recognize and understand the problem, you position yourself for meaningful change. Remember, the first step to solving any problem is recognizing that it exists. From there, you can take deliberate actions to transform your beliefs and, ultimately, your life.

**Succinct Summary**

Here's a succinct summary of the key points:

**Recognize the Problem: Identifying Negative and Limiting Beliefs**

The journey to reprogramming your belief system begins with the crucial step of recognizing the impact of negative and limiting beliefs. Awareness is the first and most important step in making any meaningful change in your life. If you don't acknowledge that a problem exists, you can't take the necessary steps to correct it. This principle is underscored in the Bible:

*"My people are destroyed for lack of knowledge."* — Hosea 4:6 (KJV)

This verse highlights the importance of knowledge, perception, skill, discernment, understanding, and wisdom. Many struggles arise not because of external circumstances but because of an internal lack of awareness. When people fail to recognize the negative patterns or beliefs influencing their lives, they miss the opportunity for transformation. As the saying goes, "A problem identified is a problem half-solved."

## Understanding the Problem: The Role of the Subconscious Mind

If your life seems off course despite your best efforts—if you've done everything right yet still face recurring issues—it might be time to examine your subconscious mind. The subconscious mind runs programs based on beliefs and experiences accumulated over the years. These programs can dictate your actions, reactions, and even your emotional responses, often without your conscious awareness.

For example, if you feel anxious every time you think about finances or dread certain social interactions, these reactions might stem from deep-seated beliefs formed in the past. Identifying these beliefs is the first step toward overcoming them.

# Chapter 18

# THINK GOD'S THOUGHTS

## Have the Mind of Christ

Having the mind of Christ means thinking God's thoughts rather than thinking as the natural man does. It involves aligning your mind with God's values and desires. Is this even possible? Yes, it is. The Bible says:

*"But we have the mind of Christ."* —1 Corinthians 2:16b (NIV)

Who are the "we" in this Scripture? When you read the preceding verses, the apostle Paul is referring to believers—those who believe in their hearts that Christ is the Savior and confess their sins with their mouths, acknowledging that Christ is Lord.

So, what does it mean to have the mind of Christ? When you have the mind of Christ, you can discern between spiritual matters and those of the natural man. This is crucial because the spiritual realm governs the physical or natural world. Likewise, the spiritual man governs the natural man.

Remember, we said that man is a triune being—three in one. Man is not just what we see in the physical state; he is a three-part whole consisting of spirit, soul, and body. We also mentioned that the spirit is the real essence of a person, and it plays a vital role in inspiring the soul and body. The spirit of a man determines his identity, and therefore, the nature of a person's spirit influences how they behave.

To reprogram our belief system, we must start by renewing the nature of our spirit. And you cannot renew the spirit's nature without embracing the concept of the new creation.

## New Creation Reality

The reality of becoming a new creation is one of the most profound truths in the Bible:

*"Therefore, if anyone is in Christ, he is a new creation; old things have passed away; behold, all things have become new."* —2 Corinthians 5:17 (NKJV)

What does this mean? The Living Bible (TLB) explains it this way: *"When someone becomes a Christian, he becomes a brand new person inside. He is not the same anymore. A new life has begun."* Becoming a Christian is not the same as being born into a Christian family or choosing Christianity as your religion. It's not about going to church or belonging to a denomination—whether Catholic, Protestant, Anglican, Methodist, Baptist, Evangelical, Pentecostal, or interdenominational. Becoming a Christian is far more than just having a Christian name. You can be a Christian and still never experience the realities of being a new creation. Yes, you can identify as a Christian without truly being in Christ.

According to the above Scripture, there is only one qualification to become a new creation: *"If anyone is in Christ, he is a new creation."* What makes someone a new creation? The Bible says, *"Old things have passed away; behold, all things have become new."* You become a new creation when you are in Christ, and a divine transformation takes place where the old is gone, and everything becomes new. But how does this happen? The Amplified Bible version clarifies:

*"Therefore if anyone is in Christ [that is, grafted in, joined to Him by faith in Him as Savior], he is a new creature [reborn and renewed by the Holy Spirit]; the old things [the previous moral and spiritual condition] have passed away. Behold, new things have come [because spiritual awakening brings a new life]."* —2 Corinthians 5:17 (AMP)

To be in Christ means to be grafted in and joined to Him by faith, accepting Him as your personal Lord and Savior by believing in your heart that Christ is the Savior and confessing with your mouth your sins, and that Christ is Lord. The Bible puts it this way:

*"For with the heart man believeth unto righteousness; and with the mouth confession is made unto salvation."* —Romans 10:10 (KJV)

Based on this, there are two essential steps to becoming a new creation: first, *"believe with the heart,"* and second, *"confess with the mouth."* Without these two actions, salvation cannot occur. The Amplified Bible further elaborates:

*"For with the heart a person believes [in Christ as Savior], resulting in his justification [that is, being made righteous— being freed from the guilt of sin and made acceptable to God]; and with the mouth he acknowledges and confesses [his faith openly], resulting in and confirming [his] salvation."*

—Romans 10:10 (AMP)

Becoming a new creation is the essence of salvation. Salvation is more than just receiving forgiveness for your sins; it is about becoming a new creation, free from the guilt of sin. How? As the Scripture explains, the moment a person believes in their heart that Christ is the Savior, they are justified—made righteous, freed from the guilt of sin, and made acceptable to God. Thus, in becoming a new creation, the person is declared righteous and not guilty.

To be righteous means to be in "right standing with God." This does not mean, *"I am no longer guilty right now, but if I sin again, I will be guilty again."* Nor does it mean, *"I am righteous right now, but if I sin again, I am no longer righteous."* No, the reality of becoming a new creation is this:

*"I am righteous and no longer guilty."* This is why the Bible says:

*"For He made Him who knew no sin to be sin for us, that we might become the righteousness of God in Him."*

—2 Corinthians 5:21 (NKJV)

This Scripture declares that we have become righteous, which means we are no longer guilty. It is clear from this verse that we become the righteousness of God because *"He made Him who knew no sin to be sin for us,"* not because of our own actions. The Amplified Bible states it this way: *"He made Christ who knew no sin to [judicially] be sin on our behalf, so that in Him we would become the righteousness of God [that is, we would be made acceptable to Him and placed in a right relationship with Him by His gracious lovingkindness]."* So, stop viewing yourself as guilty, for you cannot be both righteous and guilty at the same time.

While it is true that you may not live the rest of your life without sinning, as a new creation, you are not guilty. You cannot be a new creation today and, if you sin tomorrow, suddenly become no longer a new creation. It doesn't work that way. If you do sin, the Bible assures us that we have an advocate with the Father:

*"My dear children, I write this to you so that you will not sin. But if anybody does sin, we have an advocate with the Father—Jesus Christ, the Righteous One."* —1 John 2:1 (NIV)

This does not mean that being a new creation and the righteousness of God gives you a license to continue in sin. The Bible addresses this clearly:

*"What shall we say then? Shall we continue in sin, that grace may abound? God forbid. How shall we, that are dead to sin, live any longer therein?"* —Romans 6:1-2 (KJV)

However, this is not the same as the concept of "once saved, always saved." When you become a new creation, you are made free from sin and become a servant of God, called to bear fruit unto holiness and, in the end, to receive everlasting life:

*"But now being made free from sin, and become servants to God, ye have your fruit unto holiness, and the end everlasting life."* —Romans 6:22 (KJV)

But if you choose to continue in sin, the Bible warns: *"For the wages of sin is death; but the gift of God is eternal life through Jesus Christ our Lord."* —Romans 6:23 (KJV)

It is paramount that we understand this; otherwise, our minds will remain captive to guilt every time we sin, and that guilt will dictate our lives. In reality, we are new creations, and as new creations, we are meant to operate with the mind of Christ. Understanding this truth gives us boldness and freedom to control our thoughts and think purposefully. In other words, we do not have to entertain every thought that enters our minds. We have the power to control our minds because we have the mind of Christ.

## The Indwell of the Holy Spirit

After salvation, or the new creation experience, the believer's responsibility is to yield to the leading and prompting of the Holy Spirit and allow the Holy Spirit to transform his or her life. But who is the Holy Spirit? The Holy Spirit is the third person of the Godhead—God existing in three persons: the Father, the Son, and the Holy Spirit. The new creation receives this gift of the Holy Spirit at the time of salvation.

*"And Peter said to them, 'Repent [change your old way of thinking, turn from your sinful ways, accept and follow Jesus as the Messiah] and be baptized, each of you, in the name of Jesus Christ because of the forgiveness of your sins; and **you will receive the gift of the Holy Spirit**.'" —Acts 2:38 (AMP)*

You receive the gift of the Holy Spirit when you repent—that is, when you change your old way of thinking, turn from your sinful ways, and accept and follow Jesus Christ as the Messiah. At salvation, or the new birth, you receive a new nature, and to receive this new nature, you must have the Holy Spirit—the Spirit of God—living in you. This is confirmed in Romans 8:9:

*"But you are not like that. You are controlled by **your new nature if you have the Spirit of God living in you**. (And*

*remember that if anyone doesn't have the Spirit of Christ living in him, he is not a Christian at all.)"* —Romans 8:9 (TLB)

Therefore, in order to have the mind of Christ, a person must first have the Holy Spirit. Having the mind of Christ is, in essence, the same as having the Holy Spirit dwelling in you, both of which are received through faith at the moment of salvation. By implication, if you do not have the Spirit of Christ living in you, you do not belong to Him. The New Living Translation (NLT) renders Romans 8:9 this way: *"But you are not controlled by your sinful nature. You are controlled by the Spirit if you have the Spirit of God living in you. (And remember **that those who do not have the Spirit of Christ living in them do not belong to him at all**.)"*

## Partakers of the Divine Nature

Through the new birth experience, God has made us "partakers of the divine nature," enabling us to access all things that pertain to life and godliness through the knowledge of Him. As the Bible says:

*"As His divine power has given to us all things that pertain to life and godliness, through the knowledge of Him who called us by glory and virtue, by which have been given to us exceedingly great and precious promises, that through these you may be partakers of the divine nature, having escaped the*

*corruption that is in the world through lust."* —2 Peter 1:3-4 (NKJV)

The phrase "partakers of the divine nature" means that Christ has imparted His own character to us. The Living Bible (TLB) simplifies this for us:

*"And by that same mighty power he has given us all the other rich and wonderful blessings he promised; for instance, the promise to save us from the lust and rottenness all around us, and to give us his own character."* —2 Peter 1:4 (TLB)

Therefore, we not only have the mind of Christ but also the character of Christ. What does this mean? It means our new nature, through the operation of the mind and character of Christ, rewrites our old nature, enabling us to gain new desires, ideas, thoughts, and other positive qualities. These qualities can then be used to reprogram our existing negative and limiting belief systems.

Let me use an analogy to aid our understanding—think about a computer system: the hard drive and the workings of an antivirus (AV) software installed on the system. Now, consider the human being as a computer system, the mind as the hard drive, and the Holy Spirit as the antivirus software program that can be installed or uploaded into the hard drive (human mind).

In the computer world, antivirus (AV) software is a data security utility installed on a computer system to protect it from viruses, spyware, malware, rootkits, Trojans, phishing attacks, spam, and other online cyber threats. It does this by scanning files, downloads, and attachments for viruses and running in the background while the user surfs the internet. If the user encounters a virus, the program warns them and provides the option to remove it before it infects the system. In essence, the purpose of antivirus software is to detect, neutralize, or eradicate malware (malicious software) and other threats.

Similarly, once a human being (through the new birth experience) is indwelt by the Holy Spirit (the antivirus software), the Holy Spirit enters the mind (the hard drive) and can affect not only the mind but all aspects of the human being. The Holy Spirit detects, neutralizes, and eradicates harmful thoughts and behaviors, replacing them with good, functional qualities. This is how the mind of Christ rewrites our mind to make us capable of understanding and relating to God, thereby uploading and installing the fruit of the Spirit in our mind:

*"But the fruit that comes from having the Holy Spirit in our lives is: love, joy, peace, not giving up, being kind, being good, having faith, being gentle, and being the boss over our own desires. The Law is not against these things."* —Galatians 5:22-23 (NLV)

This fruit is the result of the Holy Spirit's presence within us. The Amplified Bible (AMP) puts it this way: *"But the fruit of the Spirit [the result of His presence within us] is love [unselfish concern for others], joy, [inner] peace, patience [not just the ability to wait, but how we act while waiting], kindness, goodness, faithfulness, gentleness, self-control. Against such things there is no law."* The presence of this fruit helps our old nature gain new desires, ideas, thoughts, and other positive qualities that replace our existing negative and limiting belief systems, allowing us to exhibit the mind of Christ in our lives.

However, this transformation does not happen automatically. It requires the renewing and developing of our mind to align with the mind of Christ. Over the years, we have uploaded and installed negative and limiting beliefs into our system. Since we still have this old mind, we are prone to give in to the lure of sin and the demands of our former ways of thinking.

But here's the good news! We can choose our thoughts and think intentionally. In other words, we do not have to dwell on whatever thoughts that come into our mind. We now have the power to control our minds because we have the mind of Christ. This realization has been one of the greatest discoveries of my life and is personally exciting because, as the Bible says in Proverbs:

*"For as he thinks in his heart, so is he."* —Proverbs 23:7 (NKJV)

Oh, my goodness! As a man thinks in his heart, so is he. Therefore, if I have the power to choose my thoughts and think intentionally, then I have the power to determine who I will become—for what I think, I become. Joyce Meyer puts it best: *"Where the mind goes, the man follows."* Our mind determines our ultimate outcome in life. The mind is the compass of our lives, and the way we think determine how we live and who we are. This is why it is extremely important to think about what we are thinking about. No wonder the Bible says:

*"(For the weapons of our warfare are not carnal, but mighty through God to the pulling down of strong holds;) Casting down imaginations, and every high thing that exalteth itself against the knowledge of God, and bringing into captivity every thought to the obedience of Christ."* —2 Corinthians 10:4-5 (KJV)

We need to control what goes into our minds. We need to be mindful of what we allow into our minds. It is so important for us to understand this because if we do not, we will not be able to become all that God created us to be. One way to do this is by learning how to bring every thought into captivity to the obedience of Christ.

## Taking Every Thought Captive

There are three key ways to take every thought captive to the obedience of the mind of Christ:

# 1. Renewal of Your Mind

The first step in taking every thought captive is to renew your mind and develop a mindset that aligns with God. Paul, speaking to the Romans, said:

*"And do not be conformed to this world, but be transformed by the renewing of your mind, that you may prove what is that good and acceptable and perfect will of God."* —Romans 12:2 (NKJV)

The first instruction is, "do not be conformed to this world." This phrase means, as the Living Bible (TLB) puts it, *"Don't copy the behavior and customs of this world, but be a new and different person with a fresh newness in all you do and think. Then you will learn from your own experience how His ways will really satisfy you."* So, you are not to conform to or copy the behaviors and customs around you. How can you do this? By the renewing of your mind. Your mind needs to be consistently renewed—moving away from the mind of the flesh (behaviors and customs built over the years) and into the mind of Christ.

Is this possible? Yes, it is. Those who belong to God have the mind of Christ and have been transformed by the power of the new program (antivirus software) installed when they received the gift of the Holy Spirit during their new birth experience. We have been equipped with the weapon we need to pull down strongholds, cast down imaginations, and bring every thought into captivity to the obedience of Christ:

*"For the weapons of our warfare are not carnal, but mighty through God to the pulling down of strong holds; Casting down imaginations, and every high thing that exalteth itself against the knowledge of God, and bringing into captivity every thought to the obedience of Christ."* —2 Corinthians 10:4-5 (KJV)

To renew your mind, focus on godly values and ethical attitudes. The Amplified Bible (AMP) renders Romans 12:2 as:

*"And do not be conformed to this world [any longer with its superficial values and customs], but be transformed and progressively changed [as you mature spiritually] by the renewing of your mind [focusing on godly values and ethical attitudes], so that you may prove [for yourselves] what the will of God is, that which is good and acceptable and perfect [in His plan and purpose for you]."*

Where do you get these godly values and ethical attitudes? Through reading the Bible. Every day, you need to take time to study the Word so you can intentionally think according to what it says. Renewing your mind is an ongoing process. Initially, you may not be perfect in doing this, but you have the power to do it. As you make progress each day, you can keep your mind renewed and grow in your new nature through the workings of the mind of Christ in you.

## 2. Prepare Your Mind for Action

The second step in taking every thought captive is to prepare your mind for action. The Apostle Peter said: *"So prepare your minds for action and exercise self-control. Put all your hope in the gracious salvation that will come to you when Jesus Christ is revealed to the world."* —1 Peter 1:13 (NLT)

When it comes to managing your thoughts, you must not be caught off guard. You need to be ready. That's why the Bible instructs you to prepare your mind for action. The Bible talks about the "hidden man of the heart":

*"But let it be the hidden man of the heart, in that which is not corruptible, even the ornament of a meek and quiet spirit, which is in the sight of God of great price."* —1 Peter 3:4 (KJV)

The phrase "the hidden man of the heart" refers to the "hidden person of the heart." The Amplified Bible (AMP) puts it this way:

*"But let it be [the inner beauty of] the hidden person of the heart, with the imperishable quality and unfading charm of a gentle and peaceful spirit, [one that is calm and self-controlled, not overanxious, but serene and spiritually mature], which is very precious in the sight of God."*

Remember, when the Bible uses the word "heart," it is often referring to the "mind." Therefore, the hidden person of the heart refers to our "inner person" or our "inner life." What we think about is our inner life. And as the Scripture says, the way we think determines how we live and who we are. To protect how you live and who you are, you must prepare your mind and be ready to take action against all forms of negative and limiting thoughts.

Additionally, it is not enough to prepare your mind for action; you must also exercise self-control. The Scripture says, *"Prepare your minds for action and exercise self-control."* Self-control is the ability to manage one's actions, desires, impulses, feelings, and emotions. It is about having the willpower to say no. As Bishop David Abioye said, *"The ability to say no is the hallmark of maturity."* You bring your mind under subjection and take every thought captive by saying no—and insisting on no.

Another practical way to set your affections on higher things is to have a "Daily Thinking Session." Find a quiet place each day to think intentionally. Search for Scriptures about God's love, plan, and purpose for you. Use a Bible concordance or an internet search engine to find relevant verses. Think about your current circumstances and what you are going through. Locate Scriptures that address those areas, write them down, and spend time meditating on them.

As a side note, I encourage you to post the Scriptures you've written down in places where you can easily see them throughout the day—such as on your mirror, refrigerator, or office noticeboard. Reading them repeatedly helps to get them into your mind, thereby renewing your mind with the truth of God's Word and replacing any opposing beliefs, including negative and limiting thoughts.

## 3. Set Your Mind and Keep Focused

The third step in taking every thought captive is to set your mind and keep it focused on what is above. Paul, speaking to the Colossians, said:

*"Set your mind and keep focused habitually on the things above [the heavenly things], not on things that are on the earth [which have only temporal value]."* —Colossians 3:2 (AMP)

To "set your mind" means to "think." The New Living Translation (NLT) says, *"Think about the things of heaven, not the things of earth."* Now that you know how to renew your mind and prepare it for action, the next step is to set your mind on higher things and keep it focused on what is above. The Amplified Bible, Classic Edition (AMPC), says, *"And set your minds and keep them set on what is above (the higher things), not on the things that are on the earth."* You must consciously dwell on positive and uplifting things. The AMPC uses the word "minds" (plural) because all your emotions, feelings, sentiments, and reasoning should be involved in this process. The King James Version (KJV) renders this Scripture as: *"Set your affection on things above, not on things on the earth."* The word "affections" means emotion, feeling, and sentiment.

How do you set your mind (affections) and keep it focused? By making up your mind ahead of time. This way, you don't have to wait for "earthly things" to invade your thoughts before reacting based on your feelings at that moment.

When you make up your mind ahead of time about what you will do or not do, you are laying the foundation to make the right choices, and you are more likely to succeed in overcoming temptation. This is the key to resisting and overcoming temptation. For instance, when you decide not to hang out with people who are bad influences, it will be easier for you to resist and overcome when you encounter such people. This applies to all forms of thoughts and temptations. Once you decide and set your affections on things above, you will always come out victorious—because you have the weapon to pull down strongholds, cast down imaginations, and bring every thought into captivity to the obedience of Christ through the power of the indwelling Holy Spirit. This principle even applies to small desires, such as deciding not to eat candy today.

It is crucial to think about how you will respond to difficulties and challenges before they arise. Don't wait until the temptation comes and then react based on how you feel at that moment. This approach is dangerous, and more often than not, you will struggle to resist or overcome the temptation. Unfortunately, many people fall into this trap, which prevents them from bringing their thoughts captive to the obedience of Christ.

Finally, knowing what strongholds to pull down, what imaginations to cast down, and what thoughts to bring into captivity comes down to choosing whether to believe what God says about you or to believe your feelings, circumstances, or what others say about you. Your choice should be to believe what God says. As a songwriter put it, *"God said it. I believe it. And that settles it."* When you commit to making small progress each day and set your affections (mind) on the Word of God rather than on limiting beliefs, you will be able to reprogram your existing negative and limiting belief system.

# *Chapter 19*

# VISUALIZATION

According to various English dictionaries, visualization is defined as:

- The act or an instance of visualizing.

- The formation of a mental image of something.

- To make perceptible to the mind or imagination.

The word "perceptible" means "able to be perceived; noticeable; appreciable or recognizable." In the context of our discussion, visualization can be defined as:

1. A technique that involves focusing on positive mental images to achieve a particular goal.

2. The ability to vividly imagine something before it exists in any physical reality.

3. The ability to "see" something in the mind's eye.

Medically speaking, visualization is:

- The act or process of visualizing.

- The use of mental images to influence bodily processes, control pain, or prepare for athletic or other types of performance.

This is why visualization is a powerful technique used to reprogram our negative and limiting beliefs. To apply this technique, you must focus to form a positive mental image, using it to influence your bodily processes, control your pain and emotions, and ultimately achieve any goal in your life. Through the act of visualization, you vividly imagine or "see" something with the eyes of your mind before it exists in physical reality. This is how to create a viable future.

The act, process, or technique of visualizing is rooted in the Bible. The Bible says:

*"But we all, with open face beholding as in a glass the glory of the Lord, are changed into the same image from glory to glory, even as by the Spirit of the Lord."* —2 Corinthians 3:18 (KJV)

What is it that we are beholding? The Classic Edition of the Amplified Bible (AMPC) clarifies:

*"And all of us, as with unveiled face, [because we] continued to behold [in the Word of God] as in a mirror the glory of the Lord, are constantly being transfigured into His very own image in ever-increasing splendor and from one degree of glory to another; [for this comes] from the Lord [Who is] the Spirit."*

From this translation, we understand that we are beholding the Word of God. What happens when we do this? We are constantly or progressively transfigured or transformed into God's very own image. As we keep beholding, we increase in God's splendor, moving from one degree of glory to another. By implication, the more we behold, the more glory we reflect. The more we behold the Word of God, the more we reflect His glory due to our transformation.

We become what we behold. The key to reprogramming your negative and limiting belief system and reflecting who you want to become is to continue beholding, with unveiled face, the Word of God. To behold with an unveiled face is to look into the Word with our eyes and mind open, engaging our mental faculties, and taking it in fully—just as a songwriter once wrote: "His Word said it, I believe it, and that settles it." It doesn't matter what others say, what the world says, what the history of your family says, or what your upbringing and environment say. What matters is that God said it in His Word, you believe it, and that settles it. This is the way to truly reprogram your beliefs and become what you were created to be.

No one beholds themselves in a mirror with closed eyes. Our eyes and minds are open and engaged when we behold ourselves in a mirror, so we can see the image reflected back to us. You don't look at yourself in a mirror and see someone else's image. If you do, something is certainly wrong mentally. Likewise, don't close your eyes and mind when you behold the Word of God. As you read the Scriptures, form an image of yourself based on the Word of God. As you meditate on the truth of what God says, your soul is shaped, which will ultimately reflect in your physical body, spirit, and the entire outcome of your life. Therefore, you become what you behold. Your goal in reading the Bible is to become the kind of person God originally designed, as portrayed in the Scriptures.

It's all about the mind. The images you form in your mind determine what you become. Until you can see it with the eyes of the mind, you cannot become it. This is why visualization is particularly important in life and in reprogramming your belief system. Unfortunately, many people are unable to visualize or form positive images with their mind because of the existing nature of their mind. As a result, they struggle to actualize who they really want to be and what they want to become. Jesus, speaking in the Gospel according to Luke, confirmed this:

*"No good tree bears bad fruit, nor does a bad tree bear good fruit. Each tree is recognized by its own fruit. People do not pick figs from thornbushes, or grapes from briers. A good man brings good things out of the good stored up in his heart, and an evil man brings evil things out of the evil stored up in his heart. For the mouth speaks what the heart is full of."* —Luke 6:43-45 (NIV)

In simple terms, this Scripture tells us that a good tree does not produce bad fruit, and a bad tree does not produce good fruit. Each tree is known by its fruit. You cannot pick figs from thorn bushes, nor can you pick grapes from a brier bush. The good man, by his nature, produces what is good, honorable, and moral out of the good stored in his heart. Likewise, the evil man, by his nature, produces what is wicked and depraved out of the evil in his heart. Why? Because a man's mouth speaks from the abundance or overflow of his heart, or what his heart is full of. By implication, Jesus is saying that our hearts reflect who we really are. There is no such thing as a "good" or an "evil" heart; the heart only reflects what is stored in it. If good treasure is stored in the heart, it will reflect the good by nature. If evil things are stored in the heart, it will reflect the evil by nature.

Although the "heart" denotes the vigor and sense of physical life as well as the center and seat of spiritual life, when Jesus uses the term "heart" in this Scripture, He is not referring to the organ in our body that circulates blood. Jesus is talking about the soul, which comprises the Mind (Thinker), Will (Chooser), and Emotion (Feeler). The Greek word translated "heart" in this verse is *kardia*. As I have mentioned before, and in accordance with Thayer's Greek-English Lexicon, it is translated to mean:

- The soul or mind, as it is the fountain and seat of thoughts, passions, desires, appetites, affections, purposes, and endeavors.

- The understanding, the faculty and seat of intelligence.

- The will and character.

- The soul as it is affected and stirred in a good or bad way; the seat of sensibilities, affections, emotions, desires, appetites, and passions.

By implication, the "heart" is not limited to the conscious mind alone but extends mostly to the subconscious mind. This is important to know because our lives are largely controlled by our subconscious mind. So, Jesus was referring to our mind, will, character, and the faculty and seat of our intelligence. He presented the heart as the fountain and seat of our thoughts, passions, desires, appetites, affections, purposes, and endeavors. All of these elements control our being and ultimately determine the outcome of our lives. Hence, the Bible clearly recognizes the existence of the subconscious mind and the significant role it plays in influencing our lives.

Since the human mind plays a significant role in influencing our lives, the question arises: How do I become the kind of person the Bible talks about, who has a good heart and brings forth good things, as opposed to a person with an evil heart who brings forth evil things? The answer is to constantly behold yourself in the mirror of God's Word. Immerse yourself in the Scriptures and keep your focus on what the Bible says about you. As you do this, in accordance with 2 Corinthians 3:18, you will be constantly and progressively transfigured and transformed into His very own image, from one degree of glory to another, by the Spirit of the Lord. This transformation comes from the Lord through the Holy Spirit, who will work on your subconscious mind, shaping your soul. In doing so, you will become a good tree that naturally bears good fruit, rather than a bad tree that naturally bears bad fruit.

In conclusion, our lives reflect what is stored within us, and we speak from the abundance of what we store in our hearts. That is why the Bible says:

*"But those things which proceed out of the mouth come forth from the heart; and they defile the man."* —Matthew 15:18 (KJV)

Your words come from within. Whatever word comes out of your mouth originates from your heart, and this is what defiles and dishonors you. Therefore, it is crucial that you protect what goes into your heart. It is your responsibility to guard and keep your heart with all diligence. The Bible gives a clear instruction:

*"Keep thy heart with all diligence; for out of it are the issues of life."* —Proverbs 4:23 (KJV)

According to the Brown-Driver-Briggs Lexicon, the Hebrew word used for "diligence" here is *mishmâr*, translated to mean:

- Place of confinement, prison, guard, jail, guard post, watch, observance.

- Guard-house.

- Act of guarding.

In light of this, you are to constantly watch and observe, as a guard watches and observes what goes in and out of a place of confinement, prison, or jail. In fact, you are to be the guard post for your heart. Keep it in a place of confinement, prison, or jail. The Living Bible (TLB) expresses this Scripture this way: *"Above all else, guard your affections. For they influence everything else in your life."* Above all else, guard your heart—this includes your mind, thoughts, passions, desires, appetites, affections, purposes, endeavors, will, character, and the faculty and seat of your intelligence. The power of what goes into your heart is immense—it influences everything else that happens in your life. Your subconscious mind is shaped daily by what you take in or allow into your mind. It is shaped by what you watch with your eyes, whether on television, from your computer, or in books and magazines. Nowadays, it is mostly shaped by your engagement on social media. In the same way, it is shaped by what you read in your Bible. As you meditate on the truth of God's Word, your mind is renewed consciously and unconsciously, and you develop the right perspective and beliefs for interpreting and living your life. So, be vigilant and guard your heart.

**Succinct Summary**

Here's a succinct summary of the key points:

Visualization is an effective technique that involves creating vivid mental images of desired outcomes to achieve goals and reprogram the mind. It's a practice deeply rooted in biblical principles, and when applied correctly, it can transform negative and limiting beliefs into empowering ones.

**Understanding Visualization**

Visualization can be defined as:

1. **A Technique to Achieve Goals:** It involves focusing on positive mental images to manifest a particular goal in life.

2. **Imagining Before It Exists:** It is the ability to vividly picture something in your mind before it exists in physical reality.

3. **Seeing with the Mind's Eye:** Visualization is the act of "seeing" something internally, with your mind's eye, before it becomes tangible.

Medically, visualization is known for its ability to influence bodily processes, control pain, and prepare individuals for performances, such as in athletics. In the context of reprogramming belief systems, visualization involves focusing on forming positive mental images that can influence emotions, bodily processes, and ultimately, life outcomes.

## Biblical Foundation of Visualization

The practice of visualization aligns with biblical teachings. In 2 Corinthians 3:18 (KJV), the Bible says: *"But we all, with open face beholding as in a glass the glory of the Lord, are changed into the same image from glory to glory, even as by the Spirit of the Lord."*

This passage suggests that by continually beholding the Word of God, believers are progressively transformed into the image of God. The act of "beholding" here can be seen as a form of visualization—where one mentally pictures and meditates on the truths of God's Word, leading to transformation.

The Amplified Bible (AMPC) further clarifies: *"And all of us, as with unveiled face, [because we] continued to behold [in the Word of God] as in a mirror the glory of the Lord, are constantly being transfigured into His very own image in ever-increasing splendor and from one degree of glory to another; [for this comes] from the Lord [Who is] the Spirit."*

This continuous transformation process involves engaging the mind fully, seeing yourself in the light of God's Word, and allowing that image to shape who you become.

## The Power of the Mind in Visualization

Visualization hinges on the power of the mind to shape reality. The images formed in your mind play a crucial role in determining your life's outcomes. If you can visualize a positive outcome with clarity and conviction, you are more likely to manifest it in your physical reality. The Bible supports this principle in Luke 6:43-45 (NIV): *"No good tree bears bad fruit, nor does a bad tree bear good fruit. Each tree is recognized by its own fruit... A good man brings good things out of the good stored up in his heart, and an evil man brings evil things out of the evil stored up in his heart. For the mouth speaks what the heart is full of."*

Jesus emphasizes that what we store in our hearts (our minds) is what we produce in our lives. Visualization allows us to "store" positive images and outcomes in our minds, thereby influencing the good we bring forth in our lives.

## How to Practice Visualization

To effectively use visualization to reprogram your belief system, follow these steps:

1. **Focus on Positive Images:** Begin by closing your eyes and creating a vivid mental image of the goal or outcome you desire. This could be anything from personal success, healing, achieving a life goal, or embodying a particular virtue.

2. **Engage Your Emotions:** Visualization is more powerful when emotions are involved. Feel the emotions associated with achieving your goal. For example, feel the joy of success, the peace of healing, or the fulfillment of achieving your dream.

3. **Be Consistent:** Just as with any other mental conditioning practice, consistency is key. Dedicate time each day to visualize your desired outcomes.

4. **Visualize with Faith:** Believe that what you see in your mind is already true. Just as God "calls those things which do not exist as though they did" (Romans 4:17 KJV), visualize your goals with the certainty that they are already manifesting.

5. **Guard Your Mind:** Be vigilant about what you allow into your mind. Proverbs 4:23 (KJV) advises, "*Keep thy heart with all diligence; for out of it are the issues of life.*" Protect your heart and mind from negative influences, and fill them with positive images, affirmations, and God's Word.

6. **Use the Word of God:** Let the Scriptures be the foundation of your visualization practice. As you meditate on the Word, picture yourself living out its promises and truths. This not only reinforces your faith but also aligns your visualization with God's will.

Visualization is a powerful technique that, when rooted in biblical principles, can transform your belief system and shape your reality. By consistently visualizing positive outcomes, engaging your emotions, and aligning your thoughts with God's Word, you can reprogram your mind to reflect the life you desire. Guard your heart, focus on positive images, and let the power of visualization guide you to become all that God created you to be.

# *Chapter 20*

# POSITIVE AFFIRMATIONS

Affirmations are a powerful form of self-encouragement and mental conditioning, often used to reprogram the mind with positive beliefs. Affirmation is a form of self-directed meditation or repetition. Here are three key points on what affirmations are, how to create them, and how to use them effectively:

- **Affirmations are positive sentences, short phrases, or single words that you repeat in a relaxed, meditative state.** Sometimes, affirmations can even take the form of prayer.

- **Affirmations are carefully crafted, specific positive statements that you repeat consistently over time.**

- **Affirmations are stated in the present tense using positive language, intentionally designed as if you already possess whatever it is you desire.**

This approach mirrors the way God speaks. The Bible says:

*"...even God, who quickeneth the dead, and calleth those things which be not as though they were."* —Romans 4:17 (KJV)

God calls things that do not yet exist as though they already do. This is how He created the world: by calling forth things into being through His Word.

*"In the beginning God created the heavens and the earth. Now the earth was formless and empty, darkness was over the surface of the deep, and the Spirit of God was hovering over the waters. And God said, 'Let there be light,' and there was light."* —Genesis 1:1-3 (NIV)

God created the universe out of nothing through the power of His Word. He has given this ability to humanity—to call forth things on earth that do not yet exist into existence. How? God created the present universe by the word of decrees He made:

*"By the word of the LORD the heavens were made, their starry host by the breath of his mouth."* —Psalm 33:6 (NIV)

God made decrees by His Word, and whatever He called forth came into existence. Similarly, we have been given the authority to make decrees and create the realities we desire on earth. Man has been made a king on earth by Jesus to make decrees, to create the realities of whatever he desires on earth:

*"Truly I tell you, if anyone says [makes a decree] to this mountain, 'Go, throw yourself into the sea,' and does not doubt in his heart but believes that what he says [what he decrees] will happen, it will be done for him."* —Mark 11:23 (NIV)

*"He replied, 'Because you have so little faith. Truly I tell you, if you have faith as small as a mustard seed, you can say [make a decree] to this mountain, 'Move from here to there,' and it will move. Nothing will be impossible for you.'"* —Matthew 17:20 (NIV)

The only requirement for your decrees to come into reality is faith—believing in your heart (which, as we've discussed, often refers to the mind). Faith is belief, and affirmations are one of the most effective ways to reprogram your belief system.

Understanding how this works is crucial: when you act as if you already have something, you magnetize the state of having it. Conversely, when you continually express that you want something, you amplify the state of wanting. Affirmations are an effective way to plant positive messages into your subconscious mind. They work by repeatedly reinforcing what you want to achieve, creating new mental patterns in your subconscious mind. Repetition of an affirmation changes the neural pathways in your brain. The more you repeat the affirmation, the deeper the grooves are cut into your existing negative beliefs, and the more the neural pathways in the brain are strengthened. Therefore, affirmation is one of the most effective ways to change a faulty, defective, or negative belief.

Affirmations are used in your normal conscious state—you must be fully aware of what you are doing. This distinguishes them from meditation, which involves the use of the subconscious mind.

Affirmations are most effective when they are written or printed out and posted in places you will see them regularly, such as your kitchen fridge, bathroom mirror, or personal workspace.


## Succinct Summary

Here's a succinct summary of the key points:

Affirmations are powerful tools for self-encouragement and mental conditioning, designed to reprogram the mind with positive beliefs. By consistently repeating positive statements, you can transform your mindset, reshape your belief system, and create the reality you desire. Let's explore what affirmations are, how to create them, and how to use them effectively.

## What Are Affirmations?

Affirmations are positive sentences, short phrases, or single words that you repeat in a relaxed, meditative state. They can also take the form of prayer or declarations. Here's how affirmations work:

- **Affirmations Are Positive Statements:** They are carefully crafted, specific positive statements that you repeat consistently over time. These statements are designed to counteract negative beliefs and reinforce positive ones.

- **Affirmations Are Stated in the Present Tense:** They are intentionally phrased as if you already possess what you desire. This mirrors how God speaks, calling things that do not yet exist as though they already do. For example, Romans 4:17 (KJV) says, *"...even God, who quickeneth the dead, and calleth those things which be not as though they were."*

  Just as God created the world through His Word, you can create your desired reality through positive affirmations.

## How to Create Effective Affirmations

To create affirmations that truly resonate and bring about change, consider the following:

- **Be Specific:** Your affirmations should be clear and focused on a specific goal or desire. For example, instead of saying, "I want to be successful," say, "I am successful in all that I do."

- **Use Positive Language:** Frame your affirmations positively. Instead of saying, "I am not a failure," say, "I am a success."

- **State Them in the Present Tense:** Speak as if you already have what you desire. For instance, say, "I am healthy and full of energy," instead of "I will be healthy."

- **Align with Your Core Beliefs:** Your affirmations should align with your values and core beliefs. This alignment ensures that your affirmations resonate deeply within you, making them more powerful.

## How to Use Affirmations Effectively

Affirmations are most effective when they are used consistently and intentionally. Here are some tips on how to incorporate affirmations into your daily life:

- **Repeat Them Regularly:** Consistency is key. The more you repeat your affirmations, the more they will become ingrained in your subconscious mind, helping to reprogram your belief system.

- **Write Them Down:** Writing down your affirmations can reinforce their impact. Consider writing them in a journal, on sticky notes, or in a dedicated space where you can see them daily.

- **Visual Reminders:** Post your affirmations in places where you will see them regularly, such as your kitchen fridge, bathroom mirror, or personal workspace. Visual reminders help keep your affirmations at the forefront of your mind.

- **Speak Them Aloud:** When you speak your affirmations aloud, you engage multiple senses— seeing, hearing, and speaking. This multi-sensory approach makes the affirmations more powerful.

- **Believe in Your Affirmations:** The effectiveness of affirmations is rooted in belief. When you repeat your affirmations, believe that they are already true. This belief will help manifest the desired outcomes in your life.

## The Power of Affirmations

Affirmations work by repeatedly reinforcing the positive outcomes you want to achieve. This repetition creates new mental patterns in your subconscious mind, gradually replacing negative beliefs with positive ones. As you consistently use affirmations, you change the neural pathways in your brain, making it easier to think positively and act in ways that align with your desired reality.

God's Word confirms the power of decrees: "*By the word of the LORD the heavens were made, their starry host by the breath of his mouth.*" —Psalm 33:6 (NIV) "*Truly I tell you, if anyone says [makes a decree] to this mountain, 'Go, throw yourself into the sea,' and does not doubt in his heart but believes that what he says [what he decrees] will happen, it will be done for him.*" —Mark 11:23 (NIV)

Just as God created the universe through His decrees, you have been given the authority to make decrees that shape your reality. Affirmations are a practical way to exercise this authority, helping you to create the life you desire.

Positive affirmations are powerful tools for reprogramming your belief system, aligning your thoughts with your desired reality, and creating positive outcomes in your life. By consistently repeating affirmations, you can transform your mindset, change your beliefs, and ultimately, shape your future. Embrace the practice of affirmations with faith and watch as your life begins to reflect the positive changes you've declared.

# *Chapter 21*

# POSITIVE SELF-TALK

Whether we realize it or not, we are daily influenced by the world around us. We constantly create thousands of different images from the news and movies we watch on television; from what we listen to on the radio and hear in sermons; from what we read in newspapers, on social media platforms, and in books; and from the people we meet. These images and voices sway, interpret, and influence our affections, attitudes, moods, beliefs, and ultimately, our actions and reactions to the happenings of life. Unfortunately, their influence on our lives is often negative.

Over time, because our subconscious mind makes everything we say and do fit a pattern consistent with our "self-concept," these negative images and voices contribute to our negative beliefs, creating "tapes" (a recording made on magnetic tape) in our subconscious mind. Since we do not have immediate control over our subconscious mind, we inevitably listen to these negative tapes repeatedly, causing us to live out our lives based on these negative beliefs, resulting in negative outcomes.

However, there is hope. Positive self-talk can help us overcome these negative tapes and foster positive results in our belief system, reinforcing positive beliefs. We can actually reprogram our thought patterns by incorporating positive self-talk and repeating positive affirmations. This demonstrates the power of positive self-talk.

Positive self-talk can indeed help you overcome the negative tapes that constantly play in your mind. Similarly, regularly practicing positive affirmations can help you replace your existing negative beliefs. You can also replace old behaviors with new ones. When you combine these new behaviors with positive affirmations, you can effectively counteract your negative tapes. This can make a significant difference in your life and your family's life. By being intentional and proactive in your assertions, you can create meaningful change.

So, what is positive self-talk? Positive self-talk is a compound term: "positive" and "self-talk." Self-talk is the act or practice of talking to oneself, either aloud or in one's mind. These are the conversations or thoughts directed at oneself. Self-talk is influenced by our subconscious mind, and it reveals our emotions, thoughts, beliefs, questions, and ideas. Therefore, self-talk involves talking to yourself, either aloud or mentally.

Although we are constantly bombarded with various images and voices from the world around us, no voice is more influential in our lives than our own. This is because we never stop talking to ourselves. No one talks to us more than we do. In fact, we are in constant communication with ourselves, whether we realize it or not. Self-talk is all about internal dialogue—commenting internally on everything we encounter. Whether good or bad, these are the messages we are telling ourselves all day long about ourselves. This can be a challenging battle because self-talk can be both negative and positive. It can be both encouraging and distressing. Above all, our subconscious mind is dictating the narrative we believe based on our belief system and our interpretation of the world around us.

## Importance of Positive Self-Talk

The messages we tell ourselves, whether positive or negative, have a profound impact on our lives. They can either encourage and motivate us or discourage and limit us. The things we say to ourselves about life are crucial because they shape our belief system, which ultimately determines our actions and reactions to the world around us. This is why no one is more influential in your life than you.

To aid our understanding, let's consider an example: Imagine Tommy attends a friend's birthday party and decides to entertain the audience with a joke. Unfortunately, no one really laughs, except for a few friends who chuckle politely. On his way home, what do you think Tommy will be thinking and telling himself? Is it, *"I should have just kept my mouth shut; now they think I'm an idiot,"* or *"No big deal, at least I put myself out there and tried."* This response depends largely on his personality—because self-talk is influenced by personality. If Tommy is an optimist, his self-talk may be more hopeful and positive. However, if he is a pessimist, his self-talk will likely be more self-critical and negative.

- **Positive self-talk can boost your performance and enhance your overall well-being.** When you engage in positive self-talk, your subconscious mind becomes energized, releasing strength into your body. Research has shown that positive self-talk can help athletes improve their performance. For instance, when an athlete feels fatigued during an activity, they might speak positively to themselves, which helps them maintain stamina and push through the challenge. Many athletes attest to this fact. Positive self-talk is crucial because the messages you send yourself determine whether you should keep trying or give up. These messages can either propel you toward success or hold you back, keeping you paralyzed by fear.

- **Positive self-talk can improve your outlook on life.** This is why motivational activities, such as reading wisdom notes and inspirational quotes, are so effective for those committed to positive self-talk. Positive self-talk cannot exist without positive thinking—*"for out of the abundance of the heart (mind) the mouth speaks"* (Luke 6:45). By focusing your thoughts on uplifting ideas, your subconscious mind begins to adopt a positive pattern in your thinking and outlook on life.

- **Positive self-talk can lead to lasting health benefits, improved well-being, and a better quality of life.** Among these benefits are increased vitality, an improved immune system, better cardiovascular health, reduced stress and distress, less pain, a lower risk of death, better physical well-being, and greater life satisfaction.

- **Positive self-talk can help you develop robust mental capacity.** Research has shown that people who engage in positive self-talk possess mental capabilities that allow them to think differently, solve problems effectively, and cope better with hardships or challenges in life. As a result, they experience less stress and anxiety, leading to greater peace of mind.

In practice, positive self-talk involves adjusting your language. Learn to say what you truly want instead of merely expressing how you feel. Words have power. Therefore, when something is important to you, be mindful of the words you use to describe it. Positive self-talk is not about exaggeration; it's a habit cultivated over a lifetime. It may be difficult to master if it's not your natural instinct, but with time and practice, you can develop uplifting, positive self-talk. Practice it consistently until your subconscious mind aligns with your positive affirmations. Believe that every word you speak or think has the potential to become true. Remember, God is able to do exceedingly abundantly above all that we ask or think, as confirmed in Ephesians:

*"Now to Him who is able to do exceedingly abundantly above all that we ask or think, according to the power that works in us,"* —Ephesians 3:20 (NKJV)

In conclusion, positive self-talk—what you say to yourself and believe—is perhaps the most powerful influence on your attitude and emotions. Therefore, manage your self-talk effectively and intentionally, so you can begin to live your life on a higher level, creating the life you've always wanted and deserved.

## How to Create the Habit of Positive Self-Talk in Your Daily Life

To create the habit of positive self-talk in your daily life, the first and most crucial step is recognizing negative self-talk. Once you identify these negative thoughts, you can develop the skills to flip them into positive ones. Consider the following examples:

- **Negative Self-Talk:** *"There is no way this will work."*

- **Positive Self-Talk:** *"I can make it work,"* or *"I will give it my all to make it work."*

It's important to understand and appreciate the difference between these two types of self-talk. Remember, we speak out of the abundance of our hearts (minds)—meaning, our self-talk is a reflection of our thoughts. When you recognize negative thinking, you can work to turn it into positive thinking, which will then produce positive self-talk.

However, before you can practice positive self-talk, you must first be able to identify negative thinking. According to Kimberly Holland, negative thinking and self-talk can generally be categorized into four types:

- **Personalizing:** The tendency to blame yourself for everything.

- **Magnifying:** The tendency to focus on the negative aspects of a situation while ignoring all the positive aspects.

- **Catastrophizing:** The tendency to expect the worst, rarely allowing logic or reason to persuade you otherwise.

- **Polarizing:** The tendency to see the world in black and white, or good and bad, with no middle ground for processing and categorizing life events.

Thoughts rooted in any of these four categories will produce negative thinking. Similarly, any internal dialogue stemming from these categories will result in negative self-talk. Therefore, understanding these categories allows you to shift your internal dialogue toward being inspiring, uplifting, and hopeful. As you practice making this shift daily, you will gradually replace negative thoughts with positive ones. Positive self-talk takes practice, but it can be done. It requires time and effort and doesn't develop overnight—so be patient and persistent. Interestingly, a 2012 study shows that even young children can learn to correct negative self-talk and be taught how to engage in positive self-talk.

Now that you can recognize negative self-talk, it's time to learn how to create the habit of positive self-talk in your daily life. As mentioned earlier, positive self-talk is a habit developed over a lifetime. Forming a new habit takes time and effort. According to Kimberly Holland, the following five tips and practices can help you shift your thoughts over time and make positive self-talk your new norm:

1. **Identify Negative Self-Talk Traps:** Certain scenarios may increase your self-doubt and lead to more negative self-talk. For example, work events might be particularly challenging. Pinpointing when you experience the most negative self-talk can help you anticipate and prepare for these moments.

2. **Check In with Your Feelings:** Pause during events or on bad days to evaluate your self-talk. Is it becoming negative? How can you turn it around?

3. **Find the Humor:** Laughter can help relieve stress and tension. When you need a boost for positive self-talk, find ways to laugh, such as watching funny animal videos or a comedian.

4. **Surround Yourself with Positive People:** Whether or not you notice it, you can absorb the outlook and emotions of people around you. This includes both negative and positive influences, so choose to surround yourself with positive people whenever possible.

5. **Give Yourself Positive Affirmations:** Sometimes, seeing positive words or inspiring images can be enough to redirect your thoughts. Post small reminders in your office, home, and any place where you spend a significant amount of time.

Finally, be mindful of your thoughts because they have consequences. Like the Psalmist, learn to speak to your own soul:

*"Bless the Lord, O my soul: and all that is within me, bless his holy name. Bless the Lord, O my soul, and forget not all his benefits:"* —Psalm 103:1-2 (KJV)

David commands his soul to bless the Lord and remember God's benefits. In keeping with this self-talk, he then reflects on the reasons his soul should bless the Lord: *"Who forgiveth all thine iniquities; who healeth all thy diseases; who redeemeth thy life from destruction; who crowneth thee with lovingkindness and tender mercies; who satisfieth thy mouth with good things; so that thy youth is renewed like the eagle's."* —Psalm 103:3-5 (KJV)

By implication, one of the quickest ways to practice positive self-talk is to recall God's faithfulness and goodness in your life. In other words, gratitude and appreciation are powerful tools for reprogramming your belief system.

## Succinct Summary Outline

Here's a succinct summary of the key points:

Positive self-talk is an incredibly powerful tool that can reshape the way we perceive ourselves and the world around us. Our thoughts and internal dialogue have a significant impact on our emotions, behaviors, and ultimately, the outcomes we experience in life. This concept is grounded in the understanding that the subconscious mind plays a crucial role in shaping our self-concept, which is essentially the image we hold of ourselves and our place in the world.

## The Power of Self-Talk:

Self-talk refers to the ongoing conversation we have with ourselves, both consciously and subconsciously. It's the inner dialogue that continuously comments on our experiences, thoughts, and feelings. This internal dialogue can be either positive or negative, and it greatly influences our self-esteem, confidence, and overall mental health.

1. **Negative Self-Talk:** When self-talk is negative, it reinforces limiting beliefs and negative perceptions about ourselves and our abilities. For example, thoughts like "I'm not good enough," "I always fail," or "I'll never be successful" are forms of negative self-talk. These thoughts create a cycle of negativity that can lead to feelings of inadequacy, anxiety, and depression.

2. **Positive Self-Talk:** On the other hand, positive self-talk involves affirming and encouraging thoughts that uplift and empower us. Phrases like "I am capable," "I can overcome challenges," or "I am worthy of success" help to build a positive self-concept and reinforce a belief system that supports growth and resilience.

**How Positive Self-Talk Works:**

Positive self-talk works by actively challenging and replacing negative thoughts with positive affirmations. This process involves a conscious effort to reframe negative beliefs and cultivate a mindset that aligns with our goals and desires.

- **Reprogramming the Subconscious Mind:** Since the subconscious mind plays a significant role in shaping our beliefs and behaviors, positive self-talk serves as a tool to reprogram it. By consistently repeating positive affirmations, we can overwrite the negative "tapes" that have been playing in our minds, replacing them with empowering beliefs.

- **Building Confidence and Resilience:** Positive self-talk helps build confidence by reinforcing the belief that we are capable of achieving our goals. It also fosters resilience by encouraging us to view challenges as opportunities for growth rather than insurmountable obstacles.

- **Enhancing Emotional Well-Being:** Positive self-talk can improve our emotional well-being by reducing feelings of anxiety and self-doubt. When we speak kindly to ourselves, we create a supportive inner environment that promotes mental health and emotional stability.

**Practical Steps to Implement Positive Self-Talk:**

1. **Identify Negative Thoughts:** The first step in implementing positive self-talk is to become aware of the negative thoughts that dominate your inner dialogue. Pay attention to the phrases you frequently say to yourself and write them down.

2. **Challenge Negative Beliefs:** Once you've identified negative thoughts, challenge them by asking yourself if they are true. Often, negative beliefs are based on fear or

past experiences, not on reality. Replace these thoughts with positive affirmations that reflect your true potential.

3. **Create Positive Affirmations:** Develop a set of positive affirmations that resonate with you. These should be specific, present-tense statements that affirm your abilities, worth, and goals. For example, "I am confident and capable of achieving my dreams."

4. **Practice Daily:** Make positive self-talk a daily practice. Repeat your affirmations each morning or whenever you notice negative thoughts creeping in. Over time, this practice will become a natural part of your thought process.

5. **Visualize Success:** Along with positive self-talk, visualization is a powerful tool. Visualize yourself succeeding in your goals while repeating your affirmations. This creates a strong mental image of success, further reinforcing positive beliefs.

6. **Surround Yourself with Positivity:** Engage with contents and people who uplift and inspire you. Whether it's reading motivational books, listening to uplifting music, or spending time with supportive friends, surrounding yourself with positivity can strengthen your practice of positive self-talk.

**The Impact of Positive Self-Talk:**

- **Improved Self-Esteem:** As you consistently practice positive self-talk, you'll notice an increase in your self-esteem. You'll begin to see yourself in a more positive light, recognizing your strengths and potentials.

- **Increased Motivation:** Positive self-talk fuels motivation by creating a mindset that is focused on possibilities rather than limitations. This motivation drives you to take action toward your goals.

- **Better Stress Management:** Positive self-talk helps you manage stress more effectively by promoting a calm and optimistic outlook. It encourages you to view challenges as manageable and temporary rather than overwhelming and permanent.

Positive self-talk is not just a feel-good exercise; it's a powerful tool that can transform your life. By consciously choosing to speak to yourself with kindness, encouragement, and positivity, you can reprogram your mind to support your goals and dreams. Over time, this practice will lead to a more empowered, confident, and fulfilled version of yourself.

**The Importance of Positive Self-Talk:**

1. **Shapes Belief-System:**

   - The messages we tell ourselves, whether positive or negative, significantly shape our belief system. This belief system, in turn, influences our actions, responses, and overall life experiences. Positive self-talk encourages and motivates us, while negative self-talk can discourage and limit us.

2. **Boosts Performance and Well-Being:**

   - Positive self-talk has been shown to boost performance, particularly in athletes, by providing mental and physical stamina. It helps individuals persevere through challenges and maintain motivation.

3. **Improves Outlook on Life:**

   - Engaging in positive self-talk fosters positive thinking, which enhances our outlook on life. Focusing on uplifting ideas reshapes our subconscious mind, leading to a more optimistic perspective.

4. **Promotes Health Benefits:**

   - Positive self-talk is linked to numerous health benefits, including improved immune function, better cardiovascular health, reduced stress, and enhanced overall well-being.

5. **Develops Mental Resilience:**

   - Individuals who practice positive self-talk tend to have stronger mental capacities, enabling them to solve problems more effectively and cope with life's challenges, thereby reducing the negative effects of stress and anxiety.

**Practical Application of Positive Self-Talk:**

- **Adjust Language:**

  - Practice speaking what you want to happen, rather than focusing on how you currently feel. Words are powerful, so choose them carefully.

- **Consistency:**

  - Positive self-talk is a habit that requires consistent practice. Over time, this practice will align your subconscious mind with your positive affirmations, helping you achieve your desired outcomes.

Positive self-talk is a powerful influence on your attitude and emotions. By managing your self-talk effectively, you can elevate your life, aligning your actions with the life you desire and deserve.

This approach emphasizes that the way we speak to ourselves can either build us up or tear us down. By cultivating positive self-talk, we empower ourselves to live fuller, more successful lives.

## How do I create the habit of positive self-talk in my daily life?

To create the habit of positive self-talk in your daily life, it's essential to recognize and address negative self-talk first. Once you become aware of negative thoughts, you can gradually replace them with positive ones, transforming your internal dialogue and ultimately your belief system. Here's a step-by-step guide to help you develop this habit:

### 1. Recognize Negative Self-Talk

- **Personalizing:** Notice if you tend to blame yourself for everything.

- **Magnifying:** Identify when you focus only on the negative aspects of a situation.

- **Catastrophizing:** Be aware if you always expect the worst and disregard logic.

- **Polarizing:** Check if you see things in black and white, with no middle ground.

Understanding these categories helps you catch negative thoughts as they occur.

### 2. Flip Negative Thoughts

- Replace negative self-talk with positive alternatives:

- **Negative:** "There is no way this will work."
- **Positive:** "I can make it work," or "I will give it my all to make it work."

## 3. Develop the Habit of Positive Self-Talk

Follow these practical tips to integrate positive self-talk into your daily routine:

- **Identify Triggers:**

  - Recognize situations that lead to negative self-talk (e.g., work stress) so you can anticipate and prepare to counteract them with positive thoughts.

- **Check Your Feelings:**

  - Regularly pause during stressful situations to assess your self-talk. If it's negative, consciously shift it to something positive.

- **Find Humor:**

  - Use laughter to relieve stress and reset your mindset. Watch something funny or find humor in everyday situations to boost positive thinking.

- **Surround Yourself with Positivity:**

  - Choose to be around positive people who uplift you, as their energy and outlook can influence your own.

- **Use Positive Affirmations:**

  - Place positive reminders where you'll see them often. Affirmations and inspiring images can help redirect your thoughts.

## 4. Practice Gratitude and Appreciation

- Reflect on God's goodness and past blessings as a way to cultivate positive self-talk. Like David in Psalm 103, remind yourself of reasons to be grateful, which reinforces a positive outlook.

## 5. Commit to the Process

- Understand that forming the habit of positive self-talk takes time and persistence. It's a lifelong practice, but with consistent effort, it will become second nature.

By following these steps, you can create a lasting habit of positive self-talk that not only transforms your mindset but also enhances your overall well-being.

# *Chapter 22*

# GRATITUDE AND APPRECIATION

Gratitude is a powerful way to reprogram our belief system. It is an emotion that stems from positive feelings and experiences, reinforcing our beliefs, especially when emotions are involved. This is why it is crucial to pay close attention to the virtue of gratitude. Gratitude can manifest in three forms:

- **Emotion:** A feeling of happiness that arises from appreciation.

- **Mood:** A state of mind or feeling, which is a choice. You have the control to choose whether to be appreciative or otherwise. When you are in a grateful mood, grateful emotions are more likely to be present.

- **Personality:** A visible trait of one's character, expressed through attitudes and actions. Those with a grateful personality are more likely to experience grateful moods and emotions.

So, what is gratitude? Gratitude is not just about feeling thankful when you receive a gift or something wonderful happens. It is a state of mind—a practice of pausing, taking inventory, and appreciating what is already there. In essence:

- **Gratitude is an expression of thanks and appreciation.**

- **Gratitude is a feeling of being thankful and appreciative.**

- **Gratitude is the act of giving thanks, especially to God.**

As King David said in the Psalms:

*"I will give thanks to you, Lord, with all my heart; I will tell of all your wonderful deeds."* —Psalm 9:1 (NIV)

Thanksgiving comes from the heart because it is a state of mind. To change your belief system and feed new information into yourself, free your mind and be grateful for all that you have. Gratitude isn't limited to moments of gain; it's also important when you experience loss. As Bishop Dr. David Oyedepo of Winners Chapel International Worldwide wisely said, *"If you have lost anything, God is the reason you have not lost everything."* So, be grateful.

The sense and feel of gratitude are powerful forces that can attract what you desire and alleviate the pressure and stress that arise from what you need. Therefore, practice gratitude as often as you can. Yes, gratitude can be practiced! It is a skill that can be trained. With practice and the right perspective, you will always find many things to be grateful for.

There are thousands of studies showing that feeling and expressing gratitude improves mental, physical, and relational well-being. Remarkably, countless studies have shown that gratitude actually makes people healthier. The scientifically proven benefits of gratitude are extensive. Among other things, gratitude can improve health, boost the immune system, lower blood pressure, increase energy, enhance sleep quality and quantity, increase resilience, improve relationships, foster patience, and increase overall happiness.

**Benefits of Gratitude:**

In the context of reprogramming a negative belief system, here are six reasons why gratitude is essential:

1. **Reduces Toxic Emotions:** Gratitude reduces a multitude of toxic emotions and banishes negative feelings—ranging from envy to resentment, frustration, and regret. Positive emotions replace negative ones, increasing happiness and reducing depression.

2. **Elevates Positive Mood:** Gratitude elevates your mood, helping you see things through a lens of gratitude and putting things in the right perspective.

3. **Increases Positive Emotions:** Gratitude increases positive emotions. The more you show gratitude, the more you generate positive feelings.

4. **Boosts Optimism:** Gratitude increases optimism, leading to happiness and joy. Increased optimism helps you maintain a hopeful outlook on the future and the world around you, creating a tendency to expect the best possible outcomes.

5. **Enhances Generosity and Forgiveness:** Showing gratitude makes you more generous, compassionate, and forgiving. Unforgiveness is a major cause of negative emotions because it holds onto past grudges or lingering anger. Gratitude can help you let go of unforgiveness.

6. **Reduces Loneliness:** Gratitude helps you feel less lonely. Loneliness can lead to negative self-talk, which can result in a negative belief system.

One reason people struggle to get rid of their negative belief systems is ingratitude. When faced with hardships and challenges, they often fall into a state of self-pity or feel sorry for themselves. This is why we often hear the advice: *"Stop feeling sorry for yourself."* While it can be difficult to avoid self-pity entirely, those who practice positive self-talk choose to replace self-pity with gratitude. Why? Because gratitude transforms. Whether you keep a gratitude journal where you write down reasons to be thankful each day, or you take a moment to silently acknowledge all that you are grateful for, expressing gratitude can transform your life.

## An Expression of Autonomy

Gratitude is an expression of your autonomy. Autonomy refers to independence in one's thoughts or actions. Therefore, gratitude is a matter of will, thoughts, and actions. It is something only you can decide to express. Gratitude stems from the mind, and no one can force you to be genuinely grateful. Gratitude cannot be requested, demanded, or coerced; it can only be given. For example, parents can prompt their child to say "thank you," but if it doesn't come from the child's mind, the gesture is meaningless. Thus, gratitude is meant to be a gift, not an exchange—because a gift is something given voluntarily, without expecting anything in return. A gift is intended to show favor and honor toward someone, and this is precisely how we should view gratitude.

Gratitude is a choice. Like every other virtue, it is a personal expression that stems from moral excellence, aligning our life and conduct with ethical principles. Through gratitude, we choose to celebrate rather than resent what is. Gratitude allows you to appreciate what you have, rather than focusing on what you lack. If you are preoccupied with what you don't have, it becomes difficult to express gratitude. In fact, gratitude is meant to be the opposite—by appreciating what you have, you multiply the good in your life. Gratitude is the expression of satisfaction we derive from all that we possess. It is the virtue of rejoicing in what is, not what is not. However, this doesn't mean you cannot express appreciation for what is yet to come. Expressing gratitude for what is yet to be is one of the quickest ways to realize your desires. For instance, I express gratitude to God for what I desire, trusting it will come to fruition, in line with Philippians 4:6:

*"Do not be anxious or worried about anything, but in everything [every circumstance and situation] by prayer and petition with thanksgiving, continue to make your [specific] requests known to God."* —Philippians 4:6 (AMP)

Marcus Tullius Cicero, the Roman philosopher, aptly stated, *"Gratitude is not only the greatest of the virtues but the parent of all others."* This is well said, as I believe that without the virtue of gratitude, our other ethical principles lack personal fulfillment and substance.

Gratitude is the opposite of regret. Regret is a feeling of sadness, sorrow, guilt, or shame for what has happened. It is also a feeling of nostalgia, a longing for a past that is already gone, and a desire to return to an earlier time in life. Regret originates from our belief system and is an expression of our sense of loss, disappointment, and dissatisfaction, leading to destructive emotions. The good news is that gratitude counters regret. Gratitude is an effective antidote to many destructive emotions. For example, it is impossible to be hateful while being grateful. When you are genuinely grateful, it becomes impossible to harbor feelings of hate, anger, or fear.

## How to Cultivate an Attitude of Gratitude

As mentioned earlier, gratitude can be practiced and developed, much like a skill. You can train yourself to be more grateful, thereby increasing your tendency to express gratitude. Here are seven key steps you can take to cultivate an attitude of gratitude:

## 1. Think Deeply and Reflect

One of the main reasons people struggle with gratitude is that they don't take the time to think deeply about their lives and experiences. If you can learn to reflect, you will always find reasons to be grateful. Many people are not "thankful" because they are not "thinkful." For example, consider the time when God saved you from an accident or a close call that could have ended differently. Think about that classmate who tragically passed away while you were still in primary school. Reflect on these moments—*Think, think, think,* and you will find yourself becoming more thankful.

No matter how good or bad you think life is, there is someone somewhere fighting to stay alive. So, at the very least, be thankful for your life. Life is the greatest gift of all—it is not the least. As King David said:

*"Let them give thanks to the Lord for his unfailing love and his wonderful deeds for mankind. Let them sacrifice thank offerings and tell of his works with songs of joy."* —Psalm 107:21-22 (NIV)

Give thanks to God for His unfailing love towards you. He kept you alive, and that's why you are still here.

There are countless things you can be grateful for if you take the time to think about them. Remember the friend who helped you succeed in mathematics during college, without whom you might not have graduated. Be thankful for that friend. Recall the teacher who believed in you—the one who helped you become the person you are today. Reflect on these individuals and their impact on your life and express your gratitude.

Start by saying "thank you" to those who have shown you kindness and favor. Additionally, thank God for the gift of life. Embrace awe in your life, savor it, and enjoy acknowledging the blessings you have received. This is how you can increase your sense of gratitude.

## 2. Think of the Things You Have Taken for Granted

This is another important reason to be grateful. There are countless things in life that we often take for granted. Have you ever paused to think about all the things that make your life infinitely better, yet you simply overlook or feel entitled to? Consider the following:

- The ability to breathe in and out without difficulty.

- Access to clean drinking water, fresh food, and three meals a day.

- A roof over your head and a warm, quiet place to sleep.

- Electricity, lights, air conditioning, and access to the Internet.

- Good health and fitness.

- The joy of laughter, jokes, and a sense of humor.

- The love and support of family and friends.

- The ability to walk, jump, and run.

- Your memory, literacy, and mental sharpness.

- The enjoyment of music, singing, dancing, and fun activities.

- The beauty of art and creativity.

- The splendor of the sunrise, sunset, moonrise, and stars.

- The wonders of the weather—summer, snow, blue skies, gentle rains, and rainbows.

- The serenity of beaches, forests, mountains, birds, and all the beauty of nature.

Take a moment each day to practice the virtue of gratitude by counting your blessings and reflecting on the many things you may have taken for granted. For me, these are privileges and blessings from God—not because of anything we have done, but because we have been qualified by Him:

*"And giving joyful thanks to the Father, who has qualified you to share in the inheritance of his holy people in the kingdom of light."* —Colossians 1:12 (NIV)

## 3. Start the Day with a Gratitude Exercise

The Bible instructs us:

*"Enter his gates with thanksgiving and his courts with praise; give thanks to him and praise his name. For the Lord is good and his love endures forever; his faithfulness continues through all generations."* —Psalm 100:4-5 (NIV)

The best way to start your day is with God—entering His presence with thanksgiving and praise. Many people search for ways to start their morning right because the way you begin your day sets the tone for the rest of it. The Bible offers a powerful recommendation:

*"O God, thou art my God; early will I seek thee: my soul thirsteth for thee, my flesh longeth for thee in a dry and thirsty land, where no water is; Because thy lovingkindness is better than life, my lips shall praise thee. Thus will I bless thee while I live: I will lift up my hands in thy name. My soul shall be satisfied as with marrow and fatness; and my mouth shall praise thee with joyful lips: When I remember thee upon my*

*bed, and meditate on thee in the night watches. Because thou hast been my help, therefore in the shadow of thy wings will I rejoice."* —Psalm 63:1, 2-7 (KJV)

No matter how good or bad your night or your life has been, wake up each day and be thankful for life. Somewhere, someone is fighting for survival, clinging to life on a hospital bed, while here you are, full of life, breathing unaided. What will you say to the One who gives you life? King David expressed it perfectly: *"...early will I seek thee."* The word "early" here refers to the morning, making it clear that the best way to start your day is with thanksgiving.

Begin your day filled with gratitude by taking few moments to say gratitude affirmations—such as *"Thank you for this new day,"* or *"Thank you for making me see this new day,"* or *"I'm grateful for this new chance to live my life."* A songwriter expressed it beautifully:

*"Anytime I see another breaking of day, I say thank you, Lord. Thank you, God. Whenever I see another breaking of the day, I say thank you, Lord. I love you, Lord."*

This can take just a few minutes or longer; the key is to make it a habit. Let it become a routine, and it will develop into a powerful daily exercise that boosts your gratitude and happiness. Just as you may have a habit of physical exercise in the morning, also develop the habit of a daily gratitude exercise. By doing so, you can significantly increase your sense of gratitude.

## 4. Keep a Gratitude Journal

Gratitude has the power to transform your life. When you practice gratitude daily, it's incredible how it changes your outlook and experiences. Many people keep a gratitude journal or notebook, where they write down reasons to be thankful each day. I challenge you to try this, and you'll be amazed at the wonderful results and transformations you'll start to experience in your life.

Each night, before you go to sleep, take a moment to review the day and give thanks for all the good that came your way—both big and small. There are countless things to be thankful for each day. If you take the time to reflect, you'll always find something to be grateful for.

When you're tempted to think there's nothing to be grateful for, consider the things you've taken for granted, like clean drinking water, three meals a day, a roof over your head, a warm, quiet place to sleep, electricity, lights, and access to the Internet. Take a moment to realize how fortunate you are to have these things. Many people in various parts of the world lack access to what we often consider basic necessities.

Another way to practice gratitude is by using a gratitude index card. At the beginning of each day, take an index card and write at the top: "Today, these are the things I'm grateful for," and carry it with you. Throughout the day, as you go through your activities, jot down the things you're thankful for.

You can even make this a family activity. Encourage each family member to create their own gratitude index card. At the end of the day, during dinner, review these cards as a family. Each person can share what they wrote, which not only fosters gratitude but also strengthens family bonds and teaches children the importance of being thankful.

## 5. Turn Negativity into Positivity

Negativity is one of the biggest barriers to gratitude. Some people are so focused on the negative that they can't or won't see the positive, even when it's right in front of them. As long as you're on earth, negativity will exist, but your willingness and ability to turn negativity into positivity is the key to increasing your gratitude. As Douglas Wood wisely said:

*"The heart that gives thanks is a happy one, for we cannot feel thankful and unhappy at the same time."*

Gratitude is a choice. In the midst of negativity, choose to see the positive, which will foster gratitude. It's impossible to express gratitude while dwelling in negativity and unhappiness. That's why you need to transform negativity into positivity to experience happiness—because you can't feel thankful and unhappy at the same time. Positivity and happiness are natural outcomes of expressing gratitude.

Stop dwelling on what you don't have—it only leads to depression, negative self-talk, and a negative belief system. The highest form of thought is gratitude, and gratitude is the essence of happiness. The fastest way to get rid of negative thoughts is to be thankful. Oprah Winfrey once said:

*"Be thankful for what you have; you'll end up having more. If you concentrate on what you don't have, you will never, ever have enough."*

Gratitude is the key to unlocking more in life. If you want more, learn to be grateful for what you have. When you focus on what you don't have, you deprive yourself of opportunities for more. To be "thankful" is to be "tank-full"—when you're thankful, your "tank" will be full. Melody Beattie captured it well:

*"Gratitude unlocks the fullness of life. It turns what we have into enough, and more. It turns denial into acceptance, chaos to order, confusion to clarity. It can turn a meal into a feast, a house into a home, a stranger into a friend."*

No wonder, through the power of thanksgiving, Jesus was able to feed a multitude with just five loaves of bread and two fish:

*As evening approached, the disciples came to him and said, "This is a remote place, and it's already getting late. Send the crowds away, so they can go to the villages and buy themselves some food." Jesus replied, "They do not need to go away. You give them something to eat." "We have here only five loaves of bread and two fish," they answered. "Bring them here to me," he said. And he directed the people to sit down on the grass. Taking the five loaves and the two fish and looking up to heaven, he gave thanks and broke the loaves. Then he gave them to the disciples, and the disciples gave them to the people. They all ate and were satisfied, and the disciples picked up twelve basketfuls of broken pieces that were left over. The number of those who ate was about five thousand men, besides women and children.* —Matthew 14:15-21 (NIV)

Thanksgiving is the application for multiplication. If you want more, apply the mystery of thanksgiving.


## 6. Show Yourself Some Gratitude

Many people struggle with low self-esteem because they lack the ability to appreciate themselves. They look at their lives, focusing on current circumstances or past situations, and find nothing to be grateful for. This is a misguided perspective. Regardless of what is happening now or what your past has been, the Bible clearly states:

*"Rejoice always, pray continually, give thanks in all circumstances; for this is God's will for you in Christ Jesus."* — 1 Thessalonians 5:16-18 (NIV)

God's will for you in every circumstance is to give thanks. Remember, appreciation is the application for more, and what you are thankful for increases. Therefore, be thankful for what you have, where you've been, and where you are—your present circumstances. When you do this, you will find that your circumstances begin to change. Don't be deceived—if you focus on what you don't have, where you've been, or your current situation, you will never feel like you have enough, nor will you be able to change your circumstances. As Philippians 4:6-7 (NIV) reminds us:

*"Do not be anxious about anything, but in every situation, by prayer and petition, with thanksgiving, present your requests to God. And the peace of God, which transcends all understanding, will guard your hearts and your minds in Christ Jesus."*

Gratitude allows you to shift your focus from what you lack to the abundance already present in your life. Showing yourself gratitude helps you appreciate all the good you have. It's important to learn how to appreciate your "past-self," your "present-self," and your "future-self."

Here's how to do it: when your "present-self" benefits from something your "past-self" did, take a moment to thank your "past-self." For example, if you find a meal you previously prepared when you're hungry, thank your "past-self" for making it.

Similarly, when your "present-self" takes steps that will benefit your "future-self," thank your "present-self." If you're working towards a fitness goal, for instance, each time you complete a workout, visualize your "future-self" thanking your "present-self" for the effort. This practice helps you stay motivated and reinforces your belief in achieving your goals.

In summary, you can live your best life by practicing gratitude daily. The secret to your future is hidden in your daily routine. Cultivate the art of gratitude, and your future will be bright.

## 7. Develop a Positive Mindset

Developing a positive mindset is one of the quickest ways to replace limiting or negative beliefs and helps you cultivate an attitude of gratitude. It means intentionally seeing the positive in every situation, circumstance, and experience. This is crucial because the human mind has a natural tendency to focus on the negative aspects of life. Instead of practicing gratitude, we often dwell on what's wrong, overlooking the good.

Over the years, your mind may have been conditioned to focus on negative and limiting beliefs. This conditioning makes your mind constantly look for what could limit or hurt you, magnifying the bad and empowering the negative. For instance, when you look in the mirror, you might immediately notice your perceived flaws instead of appreciating your beautiful features. But here's the truth: you have the power to choose what you focus on. Negatives are always available, but so are positives. Why not focus on the positive?

When you focus on the positive, you radiate confidence and attract positivity to yourself and others. Choosing positivity, gratitude, and appreciation over negativity, ingratitude, and criticism leads to attracting more of the positive things you can appreciate and be grateful for.

To overcome limiting, negative, and self-sabotaging beliefs, you need to develop a positive mindset. Start by creating a list of things you are grateful for in your life. Each time your mind gravitates towards the negative aspects of a situation, flip your thoughts to the items on your gratitude list. Remember, your mind is operating based on the limiting and negative belief systems that have been stored over the years. Ask yourself, "Does this belief move me along the path of gratitude, or does it hold me back?" Your answer should always lead you to choose the path of gratitude.

By doing this, you are training your mind to focus on empowering beliefs. It won't be easy at first, but with practice and diligence, you'll find that adopting a positive mindset and cultivating an attitude of gratitude will become more natural to you.

## Succinct Summary

Gratitude is a powerful tool for reprogramming your belief system and creating a more positive and fulfilling life. Here's a breakdown of how gratitude works and why it's essential:

## The Nature of Gratitude

Gratitude is not just a fleeting emotion when something good happens; it's a comprehensive state of mind that influences your overall outlook on life. It manifests in three forms:

1. **Emotion:** A feeling of happiness that arises from appreciation.

2. **Mood:** A state of mind that you can choose, leading to a consistent sense of thankfulness.

3. **Personality:** A trait that reflects in your behavior, making gratitude a natural part of your character.

## Understanding Gratitude

Gratitude involves pausing to appreciate what you have, rather than focusing solely on what you want or lack. It's about recognizing the value in both big and small aspects of life, whether it's something you've gained or something you've lost.

## Gratitude is:

- An expression of thanks and appreciation.

- A feeling of being thankful and appreciative.

- The act of giving thanks, especially to God.

King David encapsulated this beautifully in Psalm 9:1 (NIV): *"I will give thanks to you, Lord, with all my heart; I will tell of all your wonderful deeds."*

## The Power of Gratitude

Gratitude is a transformative force that can reprogram your belief system and positively impact every area of your life. It's not just about feeling good; it's about creating a foundation for a healthier, happier, and more resilient mindset.

## Gratitude as a Remedy for Negative Beliefs

Ingratitude can trap you in negative belief systems, especially when faced with hardships. Self-pity and focusing on what's wrong can reinforce negative thoughts and emotions. However, by choosing gratitude, you can break this cycle.

Gratitude is a transformative force that can reprogram your belief system, leading to a more positive, healthy, and fulfilling life. By consciously practicing gratitude, you can replace negative emotions with positive ones, fostering a mindset that attracts more of what you desire and helps you navigate life's challenges with grace and resilience.

# Chapter 23

# CREATE A VISION BOARD (DREAM BOARD)

Creating a vision board, also known as a dream board, is a powerful way to reprogram your belief system and manifest your goals. A vision board is a collage of images, pictures, text, words, and affirmations that represent your dreams, goals, ambitions, and desires. It serves as a visual tool to help you focus on specific aspirations, providing inspiration and motivation. It serves as a visual representation of your dreams, goals, ambitions, and desires, helping you to focus on and manifest what you want in life.

**The Biblical Foundation for a Vision Board**

The concept of a vision board is rooted in Biblical principles. God instructed the prophet Habakkuk:

*"Then the Lord answered me and said: 'Write the vision And make it plain on tablets, That he may run who reads it. For the vision is yet for an appointed time; But at the end it will speak,*

*and it will not lie. Though it tarries, wait for it; Because it will surely come, It will not tarry.'"* —Habakkuk 2:2-3 (NKJV)

This scripture highlights the importance of making your vision clear and tangible. By creating a vision board, you give physical form to your dreams and aspirations, making them easier to visualize and work toward.

## How a Vision Board Reprograms Your Belief System

A vision board works by creating a visual representation of what you want, serving as a shortcut for your subconscious mind. The purpose of a vision board is to create a visual shortcut for your subconscious mind. While affirmations reinforce your goals through auditory means, a vision board does so visually. This dual approach helps engrain your goals deeply into your subconscious.

Your vision board should not only focus on material desires but also on how you want to feel. Since feelings reinforce beliefs, focusing on the emotions associated with your goals will help eradicate negative beliefs and replace them with positive, productive ones.

When you direct your attention and feelings toward the images on your vision board, you activate the energy of those desires within your subconscious mind. As you focus on these visual cues, your subconscious mind begins to unconsciously scan your environment for opportunities that align with your goals. This process brings those opportunities into your conscious awareness, making it easier to achieve your desires.

As Tony Robbins famously said, *"Energy flows where attention goes."* By focusing on specific desires, you channel your energy towards achieving them, which in turn reprograms your belief system.

**Steps to Create a Vision Board**

**1. Identify Your Goals:** Begin by thinking about what you want to achieve in various areas of your life, such as:

- Self-Improvement & Growth

- Physical Health and Spiritual Life

- Business & Career

- Relationships: Family, Friends, and Social Life

- Creative Projects

- Finances & Investing

- Service & Contribution

Take a mental inventory of what you desire in each of these areas and write them down. Remember to focus on how you want to feel, not just on the material things you want.

**2. Set SMART Goals:** To achieve what you really want in life, your goals should be "SMART"—Specific, Measurable, Achievable, Realistic, and Timely. This approach ensures that your goals are clear, focused, and attainable. Ensure your goals are:

- **Specific**: Clearly define what you want to achieve.
- **Measurable**: Establish criteria to measure your progress.
- **Achievable**: Set realistic and attainable goals.
- **Relevant**: Ensure your goals align with your life's purpose.
- **Time-bound**: Set deadlines to keep you focused.

**3. Choose Your Vision Board Elements:** From the goals and aspirations you've identified, select the images, words, and affirmations that resonate most with you. Collect images, quotes, words, and symbols that resonate with your goals. These can come from magazines, the internet, or personal photos. Choose visuals that evoke positive emotions and align with your aspirations. The purpose of your vision board is to bring these elements to life, so choose visuals that inspire and motivate you.

**4. Assemble Your Vision Board:** Arrange your materials on a board, ensuring each element represents a key aspect of your goals. Focus on creating a board that visually inspires you every time you see it. You can use a physical board or a digital one, depending on your preference.

**5. Place Your Vision Board Where You'll See It Often:** Position your vision board in a place where you'll see it daily—such as your bedroom, office, or a prominent spot at home. This consistent exposure will reinforce your goals and keep your subconscious mind focused on them.

**6. Focus Your Energy:** Once your vision board is complete, focus your energy on your goals. Become obsessed with them in a positive way. Remember, what you focus on expands, and your energy goes where your attention flows. By consistently focusing on the images and affirmations on your vision board, you engage your subconscious mind, which will start scanning the world for opportunities to make these goals a reality. By consistently directing your attention towards your vision board, you will:

- Gain insights, understanding, and discernment that were previously unavailable.

- Encounter people and opportunities that align with your goals.

- Access resources and support to help you achieve your aspirations.

**Benefits of a Vision Board**

- **Increased Awareness and Opportunity:** By focusing on your vision board, you heighten your awareness of opportunities that align with your goals. What once seemed impossible can become attainable as your subconscious mind identifies paths and resources you previously overlooked.

- **Motivation and Inspiration:** A vision board serves as a constant reminder of what you're working towards. It keeps you motivated and inspired, especially during challenging times.

- **Alignment with Positive Affirmations:** Your vision board should complement your positive affirmations. Together, they reinforce your goals both visually and auditorily, making them more ingrained in your subconscious mind.

Creating a vision board is a powerful way to reprogram your belief system. It helps you to focus on positive outcomes and feelings, replacing negative beliefs with empowering ones. By regularly engaging with your vision board, you align your thoughts, emotions, and actions towards achieving your goals, bringing your dreams to life.

A vision board is more than just a collection of images; it is a powerful tool that aligns your subconscious mind with your conscious desires. By regularly engaging with your vision board, you reinforce positive beliefs, attract the resources and opportunities you need, and ultimately manifest your dreams. As you continue to focus on your vision, what once seemed impossible can become your reality, replacing negative beliefs with a mindset of possibility and growth.

# Chapter 24

# MEDITATION

In this context, meditation as a tool for reprogramming your belief system is brainwork—mental effort involving the active use of the brain. It goes beyond the common practice of quieting the mind by focusing on breathing, a mantra, etc., for spiritual awareness or stress reduction.

For this purpose, meditation can be defined as:

- **Continued or extended thought:** This means lasting or enduring without interruption.

- **Reflection:** The process of producing an image or representation; it involves fixing thoughts on something and careful consideration.

- **Contemplation:** Thoughtful observation and deep consideration, often characterized by focused thought and concentration of the mind and soul upon God.

Meditation requires active engagement of the brain. It is simply brainwork—mental effort involving the exertion of mental power, which is accomplished through thinking. And what is thinking? It is the process of thought or reasoning.

When you think, you are engaging in conscious thought. But what exactly is thought?

**Thought:**

- To have a conscious mind, to some extent, involves reasoning, remembering experiences, and making rational decisions.

- To employ one's mind rationally and objectively in evaluating or dealing with a given situation.

To meditate is to employ or concentrate your mind and soul without interruption, engaging in extended reasoning and remembering experiences through observation and deep consideration. This process produces an image or representation of the focus.

This is why meditation plays a vital role in reprogramming the subconscious mind. Meditation helps to still your mind, making your brain more open and receptive, thus becoming fertile ground for whatever you wish to "implant" into your conscious and subconscious mind.

One of the key outcomes of meditation is the careful consideration of existing faulty, defective, or negative beliefs and replacing them with positive and productive beliefs.

## Engage the Power of the Mind

Our minds are incredibly powerful, and our thoughts shape who we are and who we will become. In the book of Deuteronomy, God says:

*"This day I call the heavens and the earth as witnesses against you that I have set before you life and death, blessings and curses. Now choose life, so that you and your children may live."* — Deuteronomy 30:19 (NIV)

When God created man, He gave him the ability to make choices, which means man has "willpower"—the strength of will to carry out one's decisions, wishes, or plans. Remember, the soul is the seat of the mind (Thinker), will (Chooser), and emotion (Feeler). It is clear from the above scripture that man was given a choice between life and death and was urged to choose life. But because he has willpower, he alone can ultimately decide what to do. This demonstrates the immense power of the human mind.

Similarly, to reprogram your belief system, you must choose to do so by engaging your mental faculties.

This implies that you have the power to choose life, which includes the experiences of life, such as love, joy, peace, etc. Unfortunately, many people believe that life's circumstances determine whether they will find love, have joy, or experience peace. But this is not the case. You might wonder, "Do you mean that all I have to do is choose love, joy, and peace, and

I will have them? Can it be that simple?" Yes, it is that simple. This is the power of your mind.

To reprogram our negative belief systems, we must harness the undeniable power of our minds and thoughts by engaging in the process of meditation. Meditation helps us still our minds, enabling us to think clearly. In her book *Switch on Your Brain*, Dr. Caroline Leaf says, "*As we think, we change the physical nature of our brain. As we consciously direct our thinking, we can wire out toxic patterns of thinking and replace them with healthy thoughts.*" This is exactly what we do when we engage in meditation.

"*Do not conform to the pattern of this world, but be transformed by the renewing of your mind. Then you will be able to test and approve what God's will is—his good, pleasing and perfect will.*" — Romans 12:2 (NIV)

Transformation in our belief system comes through the renewing of our minds. But we cannot renew our minds without productive thinking. When Jesus came to earth, the central theme of His message was "change your inner self—your mind."

"*From that time Jesus began to preach and say, 'Repent [change your inner self—your old way of thinking, regret past sins, live your life in a way that proves repentance; seek God's purpose for your life], for the kingdom of heaven is at hand.'*" — Matthew 4:17 (AMP)

The emphasis here is on "change your inner self—your old way of thinking." To experience transformation, you must renew your mind by changing the way you think. When you change the way you think, you change your perspective, which ultimately changes how you act and react in the world.

To effectively change your thinking—your old way of thinking—you must first cast down the imaginations that shape your current thoughts and bring every thought into captivity that doesn't align with who God says you are.

*"Casting down imaginations, and every high thing that exalteth itself against the knowledge of God, and bringing into captivity every thought to the obedience of Christ;"*

— 2 Corinthians 10:5 (KJV)

You must take every negative thought captive. Capturing your thoughts requires the process of meditation. But when we don't make time for meditation, our thoughts, emotions, and feelings will continue to control us and dictate the course of our lives.

The scripture above also speaks directly to the power of our thoughts. Not only do our thoughts shape our lives, but they also have the power to influence the lives of our future children and their children, as we ultimately pass on our belief systems to them. Your dispositions, bad habits, anxieties, and hatreds can impact your children even before they are conceived. This is why you should embrace meditation to reprogram your negative belief system.

As they say, "nature abhors a vacuum." Once you cast down negative imaginations and take every negative thought captive, you must fill your mind with something else, or similar negative thoughts will return. The question is: what should you fill your mind with? The Apostle Paul provides the answer:

*"Finally, brothers and sisters, whatever is true, whatever is noble, whatever is right, whatever is pure, whatever is lovely, whatever is admirable — if anything is excellent or praiseworthy—think about such things."*

— Philippians 4:8 (NIV)

The word "think" in the phrase "...think about such things" actually means "meditate." Here's how the New King James Version renders this scripture:

*"Finally, brethren, whatever things are true, whatever things are noble, whatever things are just, whatever things are pure, whatever things are lovely, whatever things are of good report, if there is any virtue and if there is anything praiseworthy— meditate on these things."*

— Philippians 4:8 (NKJV)

Folks, whatever is noble, right, pure, lovely, admirable, true, excellent, or praiseworthy—meditate on these things. Every now and then, we meet someone who stands out. When you encounter them, you can sense that they are different. They are calm, unshaken by life's challenges, with an attractive personality and beliefs. They are almost impossible to offend, loving everyone, even their enemies. Their love, joy, and peace are infectious. Sometimes, you might wonder if they have a special tonic, and if so, where you can get it.

The truth is, there is no tonic. People with a positive and attractive belief system understand Philippians 4:8. They choose to think on things that are noble, right, pure, lovely, admirable, true, excellent, and praiseworthy, thereby eliminating negativity. They see themselves as God sees them—created in the very image and likeness of God. You are created in the image of God, full of love, joy, and grace. You've got to start believing this. As the saying goes, "what you choose to see determines your reality." You have the power to change your reality by shifting your focus, changing your thoughts, and reprogramming your beliefs. No wonder the Bible says:

*"For as he thinketh in his heart, so is he."*

— Proverbs 23:7a (KJV)

What you think in your heart (mind) is what you become. You cannot be greater than your thoughts. Stop fooling yourself—you are not a victim of any biological mutation or circumstances. As Jesus said:

*"A good man out of the good treasure of his heart bringeth forth that which is good; and an evil man out of the evil treasure of his heart bringeth forth that which is evil: for of the abundance of the heart his mouth speaketh."*

— Luke 6:45 (KJV)

*"For the mouth speaks what the heart is full of"* (NIV). Today, science is confirming what the Bible has said all along. Dr. Caroline Leaf, in her book *Switch on Your Brain*, states, *"When you think, you build thoughts, and these become physical substances in your brain."* What we think in our minds determines what we become in the physical world. Whether you believe it or not, what you allow into your mind determines your reality and ultimately your legacy. It is time to start capturing those negative thoughts and beliefs, cast down negative imaginations, and bring those thoughts into captivity.

## Succinct Summary

## The Role of Meditation in Reprogramming

Meditation helps you still your mind, making it more receptive to new beliefs and ideas. In this state, your brain becomes fertile ground for planting positive thoughts and beliefs, which can then grow and flourish.

Transformation begins with renewing the mind, which requires productive thinking and deliberate focus on positive and empowering thoughts.

## Steps to Effective Meditation for Reprogramming

1. **Cast Down Negative Thoughts:** Start by identifying and casting down negative thoughts and imaginations that do not align with your desired reality. 2 Corinthians 10:5 (KJV) instructs us to: *"Casting down imaginations, and every high thing that exalteth itself against the knowledge of God, and bringing into captivity every thought to the obedience of Christ."*

2. **Fill Your Mind with Positive Thoughts:** After removing negative thoughts, fill your mind with positive, noble, pure, lovely, and praiseworthy thoughts. Philippians 4:8 (NKJV) advises: *"Finally, brethren, whatever things are true, whatever things are noble, whatever things are just, whatever things are pure, whatever things are lovely, whatever things are of good report, if there is any virtue and if there is anything praiseworthy—meditate on these things."*

3. **Engage in Deep Thinking:** Meditation involves deep thinking—reflecting on your experiences, considering new perspectives, and allowing these thoughts to

shape your belief system. As Proverbs 23:7 (KJV) says, *"For as he thinketh in his heart, so is he."*

4. **Use Your Willpower:** Choose to focus on positive, life-affirming thoughts. Your willpower allows you to direct your mind toward thoughts that will transform your belief system and, consequently, your life.

5. **Replace Negative Beliefs with Positive Ones:** Through meditation, actively replace limiting beliefs with empowering beliefs. Focus on thoughts that align with your goals and desired outcomes.

6. **Consistent Practice:** Meditation requires consistent practice. Over time, this practice will lead to a reprogrammed belief system, resulting in a transformed life.

Meditation, when used as a tool for reprogramming your belief system, is a powerful practice that can lead to profound changes in your life. By engaging your mind in deep, focused thought, you can cast down negative beliefs, replace them with positive ones, and ultimately transform your reality. As you meditate, remember that your thoughts shape your life, and through intentional focus, you can create the life you desire.

# *Conclusion*

As we come to the end of this journey through the intricate landscape of your belief system, one truth remains clear: the thoughts you entertain and the beliefs you hold are the architects of your reality. Throughout this book, we've explored how your belief system is not just a passive collection of ideas, but an active force that dictates the course of your life. From shaping your self-identity to influencing your decisions and behaviors, your beliefs hold the key to your success, happiness, and fulfillment.

The power of your belief system lies in its ability to operate both consciously and subconsciously, guiding your actions, shaping your attitudes, and ultimately determining your outcomes. The beliefs you harbor, whether empowering or limiting, set the stage for the life you experience. This understanding is both empowering and humbling—empowering because it puts you in the driver's seat of your destiny, and humbling because it reveals the deep responsibility you have in cultivating the right beliefs.

As we've discussed, your belief system is not set in stone. It is malleable, capable of transformation as you grow and evolve. The thoughts you feed your mind, the information you choose to accept, and the beliefs you decide to nurture all play a role in shaping your future. By consciously choosing to align your beliefs with your goals and values, you can create a life that reflects your true potential.

The process of changing your belief system is not always easy. It requires self-awareness, introspection, and a willingness to challenge long-held convictions. But the rewards are immense. When you take control of your beliefs, you take control of your life. You become the master of your destiny, capable of achieving anything you set your mind to.

In the final analysis, the quality of your life is a direct reflection of the quality of your beliefs. If you want to change your life, you must start by changing your beliefs. This book has provided you with the tools and insights to do just that. Now, the choice is yours.

As you move forward, remember that your belief system is a living, dynamic entity. It requires continual nurturing and refinement. Stay vigilant in monitoring your thoughts, challenge any beliefs that limit your potential, and replace them with ones that empower you. By doing so, you will unlock the full potential of your mind, creating a life filled with purpose, joy, and success.

In closing, let this be your guiding principle: Your thoughts dictate your life. Choose them wisely, believe in your ability to shape your destiny, and watch as your life transforms in ways you never thought possible.

# *About the Author*

Nick Imoru is a dynamic speaker, author, educator, entrepreneur, and consultant based in Canada. He is the President of Achievers Centre, a division of Philips Reliability Consult Inc. Nick's mission is centered on empowering the human spirit through consulting, coaching, connecting and circulating ideas and information. His goal is to inspire, ignite passion, create profit, and make a spiritual impact, ultimately helping individuals bridge the gap between where they are and where they aspire to be.

Nick holds a B.Eng. in Mechanical and Production Engineering and an MSc. in Advanced Technology from the UK. With over 18 years of experience in the Oil and Gas industry, he specializes in Maintenance & Reliability Engineering and is a Certified Maintenance & Reliability Professional (CMRP), reflecting his commitment to excellence in his field.

As the author of over 20 books and numerous articles and research papers, Nick's work spans personal development, spirituality, academia, business, and finance. He is the founder of Achievers Consult, Achievers Centre, and Achievers Publishing, all operating under Philips Reliability Consult Inc.

Nick is happily married to Dr. Margaret and is a proud father of two daughters, Nelly and Myra. His unwavering dedication to personal and professional growth, combined with his entrepreneurial spirit, continues to make a profound impact on individuals and organizations, guiding them towards success and fulfillment.

With a vision to inspire, train, develop, and unlock potential, Nick Imoru is committed to helping individuals and businesses achieve their highest levels of success.

To contact Nick or learn more about Achievers Centre, opportunities, speeches, and seminars, please use the information below:

Email: Nick@achieverscentre.com
Website: www.achieverscentre.com

# Books by the Same Author

- A Heart for God
- Operating God's Private Lines
- Growing In Life
- Money & Pleasure: Trap of Purpose
- Success Buttons for Life & Academic Excellence
- The Making of Greatness
- Your Best Year Ever
- Nothing Just Happens
- How Did I Become Like This
- Achievers Daily Tonic
- Living in His Fullness: Unveiling the Life, Mission, Death and Triumph of Jesus
- The Wit & Wisdom of Dr David Oyedepo
- The Tongue: How Your Words Shape Your Destiny
- He Has Said...So We May Boldly Say
- Kings Don't Beg, They Make Decrees
- Character: The Blueprint for a Great Future
- Living in His Light: Understanding Your New Identity in Christ
- Personal & Family Budgeting: Mastering Your Money for Financial Freedom

- Your Money, Your Future: A Student's Guide to Financial Success
- Choosing the Right Path: A Career Guide for Teens and Youth
- The 21 Life Rules Every Child Should Live By
- Saving Your Future: A Practical Guide to Financial Literacy
- The Power of Your Environment: How Your Surroundings Shape Your Life
- Think It, Do It: How to Turn Thoughts into Meaningful Action
- Adventures in God's Amazing Storybook, Part 1
- Adventures in God's Amazing Storybook, Part 2

To order any of these books, please visit:

Our online shop @ www.achieverscentre.com

or any of the amazon websites:

www.amazon.ca

www.amazon.com

www.amazon.co.uk, etc